OLIVER & BOYD

PRIMARY ART

Investigating and making in art

PIS LIBRARY
E PRIL. SCHOOL
JOSEF GALLGASSE 2
VIENNA AUSTRIA
TEL /20 31 10 NE TEL.

Robert Clement
and Shirley Page

FAC
372.5
CLE

Clement, Robert
Investigating and making
in art

DIS08791

Oliver & Boyd

An imprint of Longman Group UK Ltd
Longman House, Burnt Mill, Harlow, Essex, CM20 2JE, England
and associated companies throughout the world.

© Oliver & Boyd 1992

All rights reserved; no part of this publication may be reproduced, stored in a
retrieval system, or transmitted in any form or by any means, electronic,
mechanical, photocopying, recording, or otherwise without either the prior
written permission of the publishers or a licence permitting restricted copying
issued by the Copyright Licensing Agency Ltd, 90 Tottenham Court Road,
London, W1P 9HE.

First published 1992
ISBN 0 050 050850
Printed in Hong Kong
SK/01

Designed by Roger Walton Studio

The publisher's policy is to use paper
manufactured from sustainable forests.

Acknowledgements

With many thanks to Phil Creek and Wendy Jones for their help and advice and to the Headteachers of the following schools for permission to include in this publication examples of work by children in their schools.

Part 1 Investigating in art

Beer Primary School
Brixington School, Exmouth
Chudleigh Knighton C of E Primary School
Clyst Hydon Primary School
Cowick First School, Exeter
Decoy Primary School, Newton Abbot
East Worlington Primary School
Elburton Primary School, Plymstock
Ellacombe Primary School, Torquay
Exwick Middle School, Exeter
Foxhole Junior School, Paignton
Heathcoat First School, Tiverton
Ilfracombe C of E Junior School
Kingsacre Primary School, Braunton
Morchard Bishop C of E Primary School
Newport Primary School, Barnstaple
Oldway Primary School, Paignton
Plymtree C of E Primary School
St John's RC Primary School, Tiverton
St Margaret's Primary School, Torquay
St Michael's C of E Primary School, Kingsteignton
St Peter's C of E Junior School, Tavistock
Stoke Hill First School, Exeter
Stokenham Primary School
Stowford Primary School, Ivybridge
Stuart Road Primary School, Plymouth
Teignmouth RC Primary School
Tipton St John Primary School
Thornbury Primary School, Plymouth
West Park Primary School, Plymouth
Widey Court School, Plymouth
Woodfield Primary School, Plymouth
Woodford Primary School, Plympton

Part 2 Making in art

Barton Junior School, Torquay
Beacon Heath First School, Exeter
Beer Primary School
Brixington Junior School, Exmouth
Caen Primary School, Braunton
Chudleigh Knighton C of E Primary School
Clyst Hydon Primary School
Cowick First School, Exeter
Dalwood Primary School

Decoy Primary School, Newton Abbot
Diptford Parochial Primary School
Drake Primary School, Plymouth
East Worlington Primary School
Elburton Primary School, Plymstock
Ellacombe Primary School, Torquay
Exwick Middle School, Exeter
Farway Parochial Primary School
Filleigh Primary School
Foxhole Junior School, Paignton
Heathcoat First School, Tiverton
Honiton Community College
Hooe Primary School, Plymstock
Horwood and Newton Tracey School
Ilfracombe C of E Junior School
Kilmington Primary School
Kingsacre Primary School, Braunton
Ladysmith Middle School, Exeter
Montpelier Junior School, Plymouth
Morchard Bishop C of E Primary School
Newport Primary School, Barnstaple
Oldway Primary School, Paignton
Otterton C of E Primary School
Plymtree C of E Primary School
St Andrew's Junior School, Cullompton
St David's C of E First School, Exeter
St John's RC Primary School, Tiverton
St Margaret's Primary School, Torquay
St Michael's C of E Primary School, Kingsteignton
St Peter's C of E Junior School, Tavistock
Seaton Primary School
Sherwell Valley Primary School, Torquay
Sticklepath Primary School, Barnstaple
Stoke Hill First School, Exeter
Stokenham Primary School
Stowford Primary School, Ivybridge
Stuart Road Primary School, Plymouth
Teignmouth RC Primary School
Thornbury Primary School, Plymouth
Tipton St John C of E Primary School
Topsham Middle School
West Hill Primary School, Ottery St Mary
West Park Primary School, Plymouth
Whitleigh Junior School, Plymouth
Widey Court Primary School, Plymouth
Willand Primary School
Woodbury Salterton C of E Primary School
Woodfield Primary School, Plymouth
Woodford Primary School, Plympton

Contents

Part 2 Making in art

Introduction

To teach Art and Design well you need to understand what it involves, what you need to have available for the children to use and how to assess what is learnt and produced. To teach any subject well you need to be sensitive to the intrinsic values within that subject and to understand the purpose which underlies the discipline. In common with everything else that you teach, Art and Design does not require you to be an expert practitioner. However, you should be able to enthuse and guide the children through a series of experiences which will enable them to learn about those particular skills and activities which apply to the subject.

All making of quality depends on understanding and the ability to research and investigate. The aims of a good art and design education are to help children to:

- become visually literate and to able to use and understand art as a form of communication
- develop creative and technical skills
- develop aesthetic awareness
- know about the contribution made by artists, craft workers and designers, past and present, to the world's culture and progress.
- evaluate and modify their own work in the context of school and then the wider community.

At a simple level, in Key Stage 1, children need to be aware that art has been made in the past, by every civilisation and culture. They need to begin to think about how things are made and why. They also need to start learning how to use a range of tools and to distinguish between different ways of making things. Learning to talk about their own work and that of others is equally important.

The requirements in Key Stage 2 develop out of those in the previous stage. Children are expected to learn about and use artists' and craft-workers' methods, to experiment with tools and materials, adapt and modify their work in the light of group discussion and to have learnt to collect and organise their own information and resources to help them in their work. To enable all this to happen you need to have tools and materials for the children to use. They, in turn, need to learn about the purpose of each activity and how to handle the skills associated with each process. You need to understand the importance of resources, both in choosing appropriate objects to work from and to have a sufficient variety in your room to be stimulating and to cater for all the children's needs.

In terms of yourself, you do not need necessarily to be able to draw or paint but you do need to know why it is important for children to have the opportunity to become competent in as many areas as they are capable of tackling. You need to be convinced that time spent on Art and Design is essential if you are to be successful. Children quickly come to know which activities you feel are important. For your own interest, look around at our environment and see for yourself how often Art and

Design are involved in our lives. Most towns and cities have galleries where people can go to learn about different cultures and ways that artists see the world, or offer works of art for sale. All of our buildings, shops, transport and entertainment have been designed, built or made. From every aspect of television and the world of advertising, to signs and symbols, our lives are influenced by artists, designers and craftpeople as they have always been in the past. To bring an awareness of this to the children is an important function of Art and Design in school.

In order to do this effectively you need to able to provide the children with an insight into Art and Design alongside a growing awareness of and confidence in their own capabilities. Any successful art and design teaching takes place in the context of a planned and structured programme of learning. You need to know how one experience builds on another and how to ensure that what the children learn gives them the ability to explore and express their ideas.

How to plan and teach investigation and research and how to organise making are explained in Parts 1 and 2 of this book, but the underlying structure which links them together is important too. In order to make anything effectively, the children need to be able to explore the subject thoroughly. They need to have the opportunity to find out what makes things grow or work, gather lots of information and try out all sorts of different versions to see which makes the best answer. All making of any quality is based on sound and extensive research and investigation. It provides not just the answer to a particular problem, but lots of additional information for later use.

Drawing is the most important activity that children do in Art and Design. It enables them to find out how things are made or grow, how they look, how to explain and describe things and even to express their feelings about events and encounters. So it is important that you understand how to frame tasks which give the children an opportunity to experience all the different purposes for which drawing can be used. For example, they might use biros for quick recording in sketchbooks, to take notes for later work, pencils to draw landscape in a series of tones or pen, brush and ink for a series of plant studies. Detailed information about drawing can be found in Chapter 2 of Part 1 and in Part 2.

When you and your colleagues have written a scheme which outlines what experiences the children will have as they move through the school, you need to look at the tasks you plan to do within a year. Then you need to acquire the resources, including objects, books and reproductions of works of art and you need to think about appropriate ways of researching the subject. Having thought through the purpose of each step you will be able to assess the success of the work in terms of what the children produce, both in the depth and understanding they show in their investigation and in the finished work, if any. Knowing that a child has been able to talk about and explain what they are trying to do is important and will enable you to help the child to achieve what they are aiming for. In National Curriculum terms your assessment will be based on the evidence of the work produced at the end of a Key Stage, or the end of a year if you are reporting to parents. In order to become expert at knowing how work is progressing, you need the experience of looking at a range of work, guided by the information and examples given in these books. Just as familiarity with written work makes it easier for you to judge it against end of Key Stage statements, so looking for particular elements and clues will help you to be confident in making assessments in Art and Design.

Throughout the books in this series we have looked at all the aspects of Art and Design which you will want to know about, how they fit together, support each other or lead from one to another. Understanding and knowing about art, investigating, researching and making form the components of a comprehensive art and design experience in the primary school.

Teachers in schools in Wales will need to note the difference between the structure of Attainment Targets for Art in Wales compared with that in England. For more information see page 127 in *Principles and practice in art*.

Bob Clement and Shirley Page

Primary Art consists of the following titles:

PRINCIPLES AND PRACTICE IN ART

This book describes those general principles that determine the teaching of Art and Design: its aims and objectives, Attainments Targets, the development of image making, structure and sequence, placing work in context, cross-curricular issues, assessment and appraisal.

KNOWLEDGE AND UNDERSTANDING IN ART

This book examines the place of critical and contextual studies in Art and Design: how to use works of Art and Design to support children in their making of images and artefacts, how the study of works of art can generate reflection and appraisal, how children can be helped to understand the relationship between their own work and that of other artists working in different times and cultures.

INVESTIGATING AND MAKING IN ART

Part 1 'Investigating' describes how children can develop and use a range of drawing skills to describe and investigate their experiences and how these can be used in association with a wide range of resources to develop their ideas and concepts.

Part 2 'Making' provides detailed guidance for the organisation and teaching of a wide range of art and design disciplines, including painting and drawing; two- and three-dimensional design. It also provides a structure for the development of children's visual language and encourages them to reflect upon their making.

Part 1

Investigating in art

Drawing and investigation

1.2 DRAWING A CHESSMAN
Year 5
Pencil

1.3 OBSERVATION DRAWING
Year 6
Chalk/felt tip

1.1 CHILD MAKING A SERIAL DRAWING
Year 3
Pencil

PROGRAMMES OF STUDY FOR ATTAINMENT TARGET 1

Attainment Target 1: Investigating and making

'The development of visual perception and the skills associated with investigating and making in art, craft and design:

i record observation from direct experience of the natural and made environments

ii respond to memory and the imagination

iii collect images, objects and source material to stimulate and inform their own work.'

These are the requirements of the National Curriculum and this book sets out to show you how these aims may be accomplished. It is easy to say 'draw this', 'paint that', but what we really need to know is what we should do with children to open up for them an understanding of the visual world and help them towards becoming competent in the use of the language and operations of art. In education we are setting out to develop children's abilities, to extend their knowledge and to bring out their full potential. In this way we find each child has their own range of interests and natural skills which they are keen to follow and explore.

Indeed, in reception classes we can see children drawn to different activities, enjoying play with different interests, equipment and outcomes. If, for example, they show no interest in language we would try to find ways of encouraging them to take an active role in learning about it because we know that without that ability the child will be at a disadvantage in the adult world. In the same way, some children enjoy art and show some ability; we should be encouraging all of them to understand the subject and to appreciate its relevance to their needs in the future.

The need to teach listening skills as a part of language development is fully appreciated and taken very seriously. Looking skills need to be taught and taken just as seriously; though when 'skills' are mentioned in art, craft and design they are often taken to mean only the knowledge of and ability to handle materials and techniques effectively. The basic human skill which underlies all drawing, painting and craftwork is the ability to make sense of the visual world, to understand it and be able to record it accurately and with sensitivity (see figure 1.3).

Whatever resources you are using, whether you are working from observation or imagination, literature, poetry or music, the children need to feel confident and to succeed in what they do. This book sets out to show the contribution that first-hand experience and use of appropriate resources and strategies can play in children's development (see figure 1.5).

Making art can be very rewarding and children will naturally enjoy exploring ways of using pencils, crayon, paint, clay and other materials but they also need to learn a variety of approaches to researching and investigating.

1.4 TIGER
Year 1
Tempera
From the poem 'Tiger, tiger burning bright'

1.5 BADGER
Year 6
Oil pastel
Study of a stuffed badger with imagined background.

INVESTIGATING SKILLS

Research and investigation are the input in art, the means by which we provide ourselves with information which we can use to respond to and about which we can make personal statements. Drawing, painting and three-dimensional work are all ways through which we can express our ideas and feelings. Just as children develop language through learning words and ways of using them, so your role here is to provide them with study skills which they can use to find out about and respond to the visual world. Your role is clear: it is not to be able to do, but to be able to enthuse, to awaken interest and to focus attention. You should do so through your skills as a teacher, not as an artist. The language you use will revolve around questions which help the children to see:

'What does it look like?'

'What is it made of?'

'Does it work and if so how?'

'Where did it come from and are there any more?'

Your aim, too, is to help the children to understand and value the marks they make and be aware of and to able to evaluate their own progress.

1.6   SHOE
Year 2
Pencil/crayon
Observation/memory

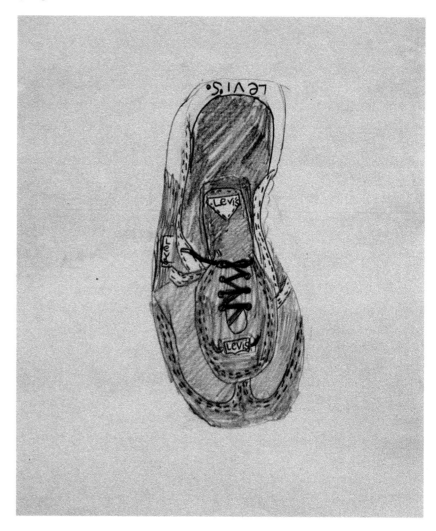

1.7   SHOE
Year 6
Pencil

DEVELOPMENT

In **Key Stage 1**, children of five and six years of age are able to draw the things they see more or less as well from memory as they can from observation (figure 1.6). You need to be aware that observation can be made more acute if you talk about and discuss the object with them, asking questions, getting them to describe, compare and look – not briefly but in detail. In this way, they can begin to find more to draw each time and the drawing will be more accurate.

In **Key Stage 2**, the need to talk in order to focus attention grows rather than diminishes. In order to draw accurately and to communicate through their drawings, children need your support in discussion and they need you to be asking questions which help them to see (figure 1.7). Once language is fully established and children can name things, the way they see them changes and their ability to draw from memory diminishes. For this reason we need to support and reinforce their looking with talk, and to do it on a regular basis. Repetition of the activity with changing starting points helps children to feel secure and confident in their own ability to achieve the standards they set for themselves. They need help to realise that they are making drawings for themselves, that practice will help them to become more confident and skilful, and that through their drawings they will find out more about the objects or things they are studying. The crucial part you play in this is enabling them to understand that to be able to draw as well as they would like will come through practice and discussion, just as expertise in any other subject is built up a bit at a time as competence and confidence grows. Children need to satisfy themselves that they have worked at extending their knowledge of the world and their ability to record it with accuracy (figures 1.9 and 1.10).

When the children can see the purpose behind the art activity and understand the opportunities it offers they are more likely to work hard and make progress.

1.9 FUCHSIA
Growing outside the classroom

1.10 FUCHSIA
Year 5
Crayon/tempera
Collage, flower head drawn by
each child from sketches made
from the plant.

Kirstin Davies

1.8 SHOE STUDIES
Year 6
Pencil/crayon/oil pastel
Memory, observation, colour,
favourite detail

**1.11   PAGE FROM A
SKETCHBOOK**
Year 5
Pencil

**1.12   FOSSILS COLLECTED FOR
A SCIENCE PROJECT**

TIME

Understanding the needs of children in terms of time is another important area to get clear. You need to appreciate why the length of time children spend on observation, working from resources and researching changes as they grow and develop. At two and three years of age children begin to make marks, as soon as they are given and can hold crayons and pencils. These marks map the movement of hand and arm and are in no sense controlled. At four and five years, they are beginning to appreciate the possibilities of controlling and directing marks and begin to make up stories which they weave around those marks.

We appreciate that it is as important to listen as to watch when small children are drawing, so the children can spend most of their 'art' time on drawings which tell stories for them. From this early stage you should introduce some careful 'looking' drawings — about three or four times in each half term — relating the things you choose to look at to areas of interest with which the children are involved.

At the end of this key stage and as the children move into **Key Stage 2**, you should gradually increase the frequency of work from observation. By Year 4 about one half of their 'art' time should be spent on observation, using those resources which are relevant not just to art but linked with other areas of the curriculum.

By the time the children reach the end of **Key Stage 2** they should be used to using sketchbooks and notebooks, spending more of their 'art' time on researching and working from resources, as this best supports their needs in terms of their development (figure 1.11). They are now fully into the stage of wanting to know how things are made, how they work and how to make their drawings look realistic. You can only achieve this by giving them an increasing amount of time working from real things.

1.13 FOSSIL
Year 5
Oil pastel

**1.14 STUFFED FOX FROM THE
RESOURCES SERVICE**

1.15 THE KITCHEN AT HOME
Year 6
Tempera

FINDING RESOURCES

Following chapters will deal in detail with the way you plan and choose appropriate experiences and resources for the children both to ensure that the tasks are manageable and that the children will succeed in the things you give them to do. But it is worth giving some general ideas here about suitable resources to use for drawing and research. Finding and using resources is actually more of a way of recognising and focusing on the environment close at hand than spending time and money gathering together a room full of rare objects. It is rather more the way that you motivate and stimulate the children into seeing afresh daily sights and objects. Whether you are in a large urban school or a small rural one, the main sources are the immediate environment, objects which relate to the work in hand across the curriculum, collections you and the children have made and any resources that may be available to you through your county loan collection or local museum.

Your classroom environment can provide you with people, furniture, walls, windows, views and masses of objects, all of which offer the opportunity to look in detail at things which relate to or affect each other.

**1.16 COLLECTION OF
RESOURCES**

Work in other areas of the curriculum – such as science, language, literature and humanities – are equally dependent upon first-hand experience and investigation in order to enrich the quality of learning. They require selected resources to bring them to life.

From early years, the children will have been used to bringing things into school which interest them or which relate to some current activity. This can be fostered and encouraged by making space to keep resources as a permanent but constantly renewed pool (figure 1.16).

It is true that by learning about anything in detail, and from more than one point of view, the experience is enriched. The children will be more likely to make better drawings, to write more informatively and generally to communicate their thoughts and ideas more effectively. An example of this might be where you take the children on a visit to the local fire station to meet and talk with the firefighters who might be willing to lend you some small pieces of equipment that you could use for observational drawing. Knowing that, say, a helmet is essential to protect the firefighter should make the drawings come to life because there would be an understanding of their purpose and significance.

Special mention needs to be made of the use of works of art in the classroom. In *Knowledge and Understanding in art* we give an insight into ways of introducing the work of artists to enhance and enrich the work that children do. Using works of art should be a part of the research and investigation you do for any project or sequence of work. It is always helpful to see how other artists have handled the complexities of the visual world and the way they used techniques and materials.

MATERIALS

We have looked at resourcing, talking and the use of time. Finally in this introduction, we need to consider materials. Whilst the choice of appropriate resources is important, so are the tools and materials that you choose to use with each one. Because you will need to use a variety of tools and materials in each year you will need to plan ahead so that resources best suited to work with specific materials are spread throughout each term. Children need to become familiar with a varied range of equipment; but too free a choice is not helpful. The discussion which precedes any piece of work or project should cover not only the resources or starting points but also what materials will best suit the subject matter or type of work (see figures 1.17 to 1.19). In a similar way, you can match appropriate materials to resources so that each piece of work provides an insight into ways of extending the techniques involved in the use of different tools and materials. You need to understand, too, the importance of choosing real resources and identifying experiences which will best match the interests of children at each stage of their development (figure 1.20). These need to relate to as many other experiences and areas of the curriculum as you can manage without forcing subjects together for the sake of widening the approach.

1.17 PLANT
Year 4
Pencil and crayon

1.18 PLANT
Year 5
Oil pastel

1.20 CHILD USING A MIRROR
Year 3
Pencil

1.19 PLANT
Year 6
Watercolour

ATTAINMENT TARGETS

In both Key Stage 1 and Key Stage 2, children need to develop their skills forming ideas from observing and recording, working from direct experience, using memory and imagination, making collections and by using a wide range of reference materials. This book sets out to show you how to structure the experiences you plan for the children so that they are building on skills they have already acquired. They should grow in their understanding and knowledge of the natural and made world and be able to explore and discover it through the tasks and experiences you plan for them. In both Parts I and 2 one of the key issues is that the tasks must be matched to the children's ability so that they succeed and make progress, and that success makes them eager to do more.

2 Resources for drawing and research

2.1 CHILDREN DRAWING SPROUTS
Year 3
Oil pastel

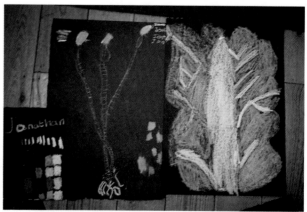

2.2 SPROUT AND CRESS DRAWING WITH PRACTICE SHEET
Year 3
Oil pastel

MANAGING AND USING RESOURCES FOR DRAWING AND RESEARCH

The effective management of resources requires organisation and structure in the choices you make, linked to the children's development through the Key Stages. In all of the work you do progression is important and knowing which resources to use and how to use them effectively is an important part of the skill of teaching art well.

In organising and collecting things you will need to take into consideration what will be most helpful for project work and to make cross-curricular links (figure 2.1). Finding and choosing appropriate resources is something that you will share with the children when they begin to work from observation and they will take part more fully as their understanding increases. One of your aims should be to help the children to understand your reasons for identifying the things they study and draw. It will help to support and extend the way they think about what they are doing in relation to their work in art. Like a giant jigsaw puzzle thoughts can relate one object to another, link experiences, develop imagination and encourage interpretation of the things we see.

The accent should be on enabling the children to move on in their thinking, understanding and appreciation of the world they are encountering. Selecting resources calls for skill in choosing the things which will most readily be interesting or exciting for the children to study and which will lead them to a greater understanding of the structure of the natural and made world.

The Programmes of Study for **Key Stages 1 and 2** move from simple recording of direct experience to enabling children to observe, select and record and to make connections between forms and ideas. For example, we might take an ordinary, everyday object, like a sprout or a stalk of cress, to see how it is formed, what its parts are, where it came from and to consider the details of its life cycle (figure 2.2). We then need to look at how this might be used in each Key Stage to best suit the children's needs.

THE NATURAL WORLD

Resources for research into the natural world occur in a wonderfully diverse variety. In Reception classes children are encouraged to explore and to find out as much as they can about the world around them. Projects and activities usually centre around the child, family, home and school. So the children will be looking at themselves and their immediate surroundings. They can make drawings in pencil, crayon or paint of their mummy, daddy, brothers and sisters or their teacher (see figure 2.3).

At this age these are most often storytelling drawings based on experiences the children have had, like playing with their friends, how we picked the flowers and, when we played with our pets. But you also need to involve the children in 'careful looking' drawings three or four times in a half term, to begin the process of observation work.

2.3 MISS CARTER
Year 3
Pencil

2.4   LUNCHBOX
Year 5
Pencil

**2.5   CHILDREN PAINTING
APPLES**
Year 4
Tempera

**2.6   CHILD LOOKING AT
SHELLS THROUGH A
MAGNIFYING LENS**

2.7   GRASSES
Year 4
Pencil crayons

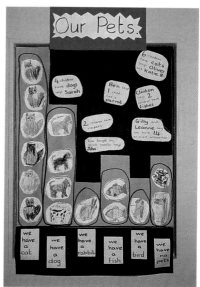

**2.9   CHART OF PETS
BELONGING TO THE
CLASS**
Year 4

These should, most helpfully, take the form of looking together at small things associated with topics of current interest. For example, you might ask the children to draw some of the apples or oranges they have brought in for packed lunches (figures 2.4 and 2.5), or some sunflowers they may have grown in the school garden. They might be going on a visit to some local place of interest, or a nature walk, where the children could take paper and pencil with them and record the shapes of three or four different leaves or flowers. Or on a visit to a beach or the countryside they might be able to bring back small examples of weed, shells, pebbles or grasses (figures 2.6 and 2.7). The important thing with small children is that they have a small object to themselves or to share between no more than two or three because they need to be close to the object and feel that it is, in some way, personal to them.

Examples of objects to use to encourage children's interest in the natural world need to have their roots firmly in familiar and everyday

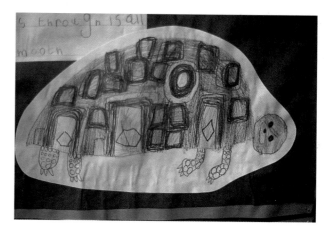

2.8   TORTOISE
Year 1
Pencil

objects; as already suggested, things such as those to do with the changing seasons, pets, food, their immediate environment (figures 2.8 and 2.9). To illustrate this we could take the example of a daffodil or any bulb or seed. In the spring, often as part of Science or as a general inquiry into growth and development, seeds and bulbs are bought and grown in the classroom. You could begin by encouraging the children to talk about what they already know about how things grow and develop from seeds and bulbs into flowers or vegetables and ask them to make very careful drawings of how they look (figures 2.10 and 2.11).

Use a coloured medium so that the children can record as much information as possible. Plant the seeds on damp blotting paper or clear sprouting or propagating gel so that you will be able to see the root system developing as well as the top growth. If you are using bulbs these ought to be in bulb glasses, as used for Christmas flowering hyacinths or narcissus, again so that the root system can be seen. Ask the children to

2.10 FERN
Year 5
Chalks

2.11 LEEK
Year 5
Oil pastel

2.12 RHODODENDRON IN BUD
Year 5
Pencil

2.13 RHODODENDRON GROWING
Year 5
Pencil

record progress every time there is a change in appearance. Again we stress the cross-curricular links here with the Programmes of Study in Science. Keep the series of drawings together and display them where possible in sequence to record the pattern of growth through to the eventual dying of the flower or vegetable and showing wherever possible the production of seeds or corms to start the next generation.

This 'series' has its own attraction because the emphasis is not on the quality of an individual piece of work but rather on the accuracy of recording and on the way the plant grows, shoots and decays (figures 2.12 to 2.15.) Thus children begin to learn not to be too self-conscious about their work but become used to sharing and seeing examples of it on display where it can be discussed and learnt from.

The same principles hold good throughout children's development but the scale of the resources need to be broadened. Instead of looking at and recording what is seen directly, preliminary sketches might be made, detailing some aspect of growth, development or decay. This is an ideal opportunity to use sketchbooks to record resources which cannot be brought into the classroom like drawings of landscapes, families, pets (figures 2.16 and 2.17), or to record things seen on a visit. Notes on colour, form and shape can be made and a drawing or painting made from sketches back in the classroom.

**2.14 RHODODENDRON
FLOWERING**
Year 5
Pencil

2.15 RHODODENDRON DYING
Year 5
Pencil

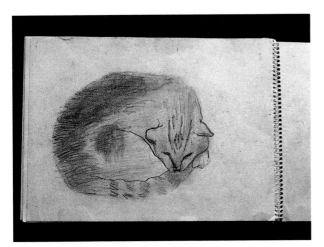

**2.16 SKETCHBOOK DRAWING
OF A CAT**
Year 5
Pencil

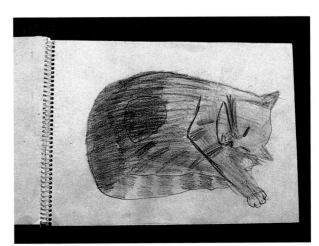

**2.17 SKETCHBOOK DRAWING
OF A CAT**
Year 5
Pencil

One possible way of extending this which might be appropriate where the children have recorded a series of drawings from growth to decay is for them to use that sequence as a basis for translation into a computer animation package. They might record the sequence and then introduce a further element using their imagination, to invent a surprise of some sort – either humorous or fantastic – like a bee visiting the flower or a mouse sheltering from the rain underneath its petals.

THE MADE WORLD

The underlying need is for children to learn about the infinitely complex world of made objects, beginning with simple and familiar things. We could take toys as an example of something very familiar and something which is of interest in some shape or form to all children.

In **Key Stage I** we could look at toys which are manufactured from natural materials found in the earth and growing on it. They are made into hollow or solid shapes which imitate real or imagined things – like tractors, trains, teddies, dolls or creatures from space (figures 2.18 and 2.19). Towards the end of this Key Stage you might go on to look at how they are made, what processes of manufacture are involved, how they are packaged and transported to the shop and the many people who are involved with all of these processes. Next comes our involvement as customers. We buy the toys, play with them, share them with friends, and sometimes give them away. They come in many different forms: individual dolls and fluffy toys to sets of things which make up a whole small world, like model railways or dolls' houses to space machines. There is opportunity here for you to ask the children to tell you all they can about their own toys and for you and them to find out from each other how much they already know about them from their own experience. All the children can be involved; all will have their favourites, and have some opinions or knowledge they can share. They can say when they play with them, which they prefer and why. In Reception classes, children will be able to compare their likes and dislikes, describe their greatest favourites and begin to develop a 'critical awareness' of the things they play with.

Clearly this analysis can be carried further in **Key Stage 2** and involve research into toys in different parts of the world. You can look at other ways of life, religious customs and what sort of toys are used in those countries. You could further extend the enquiry to look at a survey of toys belonging to the children in the class to discover their preferences. Then you could make charts, similar to those showing children's pets, to reflect findings. You could ask the children to bring in one of their favourites that they have had for a long time and weigh, measure and look at how it is made and estimate its value for money.

With all of this background involving many different curriculum areas you could ask the children to make some drawings in the light of their knowledge of the subject (figure 2.20).

2.18 TOY
Year 4
Crayon

2.19 TOY
Reception
Tempera

2.20 TRAINS DISPLAY
Year 6
Felt tip pens

You could initiate this whole project by visiting a toy shop on your own. Ask yourself which toy would interest you if you were going to look at it in detail and make some drawings. Would you choose a fluffy animal, some Lego, a tractor or a space invader? In making your choice you will have gone through the same thought processes that you are going to invite the children to be involved with and have rehearsed the type of language and the wide range of questions you will encourage them to answer in their descriptions. If all this language, thought and response takes place the quality of the drawings will be very different from a drawing made without background or insight.

Not all of the objects that we encounter in our everyday lives offer such scope for exploration, but in varying degrees all made objects can offer opportunities for visual exploration and recording.

An interesting and useful extension here links observation work with Technology in that many technological projects begin by identifying a need to redesign things that already exist. Careful recording of that existing form is essential in order to build on past knowledge and experience and produce something better. Where a need is identified for something which does not already exist, you could look at existing forms, bringing in hats, say, for the children to wear and make drawings of before 'brainstorming' individually or in groups how things might be modified, changed and redesigned (figures 2.21 and 2.22).

2.21 HATS
Crayon

2.22 HATS
Crayon

THE ENVIRONMENT

The pattern of looking, researching, recording and reviewing has been well established in previous sections. Now we look at the environment. We start again with **Key Stage 1** and work particularly applicable to the Programmes of Study which call for observation from direct experience and the environment. Again we must start close to home with work for Reception and Year 1 children and look carefully at their surroundings. Home and school need to be explored, investigated and recorded so that the children find out more as their perception increases. You can use all parts of your room, from light switches to the patterns on frosted glass, carpets and the grain on wooden floorboards (figure 2.23).

In Year 2 you can go on to making a study of parts of the school, looking at simple features like doors and windows. Ask the children to make drawings of two or three doors or windows to show how they are different from each other. You can also make use of the unusual, the things which happen from time to time which are in themselves distracting and so are turned from a potential nuisance into an opportunity. The drawings in figure 2.24 show bricks and pipes that the builders were using to add an extension to the school. The JCB excavator was a constant fascination so the teacher asked the children to make a series of drawings to show what it was doing (see figure 2.25).

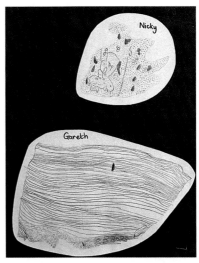

2.23 DRAWINGS OF WOOD
Year 2
Pencil

2.25 EXCAVATOR IN THE PLAYGROUND
Reception/Year 1
Crayons

2.24 BRICKS AND PIPES
Year 4
Pastels and pipes

Whatever town or landscape surrounds your school, there is ample opportunity for the children to make drawings of it which will sharpen their perception of the environment. In **Key Stage 2** you can use parts of the building such as window frames, gaps through partly closed doors or even keyholes as natural viewfinders and record what can be seen through them. In figures 2.26 to 2.28 a view of neighbouring houses is seen across the playground, a landscape from a rural school is recorded by a child using a cardboard frame to isolate an area of interest and in the town scene the children had stuck small cardboard boxes on to the window to give a 'telescope' view of the city around them.

An extended environment can be recorded using sketchbooks on visits to local areas. First-hand evidence of the past can be found in streets, buildings and churches as well as looking for sites of importance to the local community such as the police or fire stations, civic buildings and parks and gardens.

2.26 LANDSCAPE WITH HOUSES
Year 5
Tempera

2.27 SELECTING A VIEW
Year 4

2.28 VIEW FROM THE SCHOOL
Year 6
Pencil

SECONDARY SOURCE MATERIAL

Photographs, books, newspapers and other printed material, television and video all have a role to play in providing information to help us in research. With art topics or project work the children will need to use information gathered by others and learn to discriminate between what will help them in their work and that which has no real contribution to make. Activities will predominate in **Key Stage I** when you are using secondary source materials; whereas older children can use them both actively and reflectively.

Photographs are a valuable way of recording information or scenes to bring back to the classroom to work on, or they can be an end in themselves adding to material already gathered or made.

Photocopies are now widely used and make a good contribution to both observation and research. In figures 2.29 and 2.30 a fragile seed head has been photocopied and enlarged to show all the minute detail. The children drew from the photocopy with reference to the actual seed head for colour notes. Photocopying is an ideal way to capture the appearance of anything fragile and small.

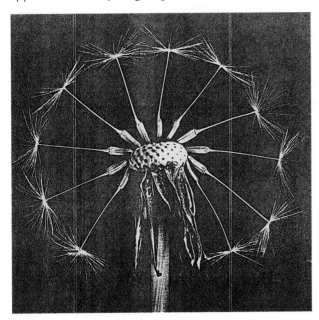

2.29 PHOTOCOPY OF A DANDELION HEAD

2.30 DANDELION SEEDS
Oil pastel

2.31 THE SNOWMAN
Year 2
Charcoal and chalks

Books are widely used in project work and are there primarily for us to read and use the information they contain. Most are illustrated and we need to be aware that many of the pictures were drawn by illustrators of our own time, working on a commercial basis, with no more access to the real things they are illustrating than we have. Illustrations are only useful if they add to our knowledge of the subject in some way.

Books also offer us powerful images which capture children's imagination and we should incorporate these into our cross-curricular work. For example, Raymond Briggs' *The Snowman* is very popular and children in both Key Stages would respond well to working from this type of source material (figures 2.31 and 2.32) either by using the existing image that they know and enjoy or by making up one of their own to illustrate a story they might have written on a similar subject. Children can also be encouraged to extend their thinking about the stories they read and to imagine themselves involved with the action. In figure 2.33 the children have been reading a story about a witch who cast magic spells on people and they have made drawings to show what they thought they might have been turned into, in a series of stages.

2.32 CHRISTMAS MESSAGE
Year 4
Crayon and pastel

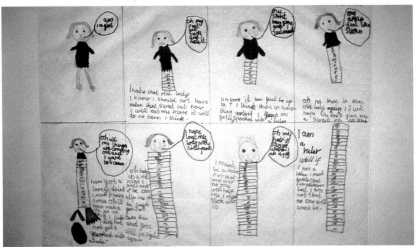

2.33 METAMORPHOSIS
Year 3
Biro and crayon
Girl changing into a ruler.

Newspapers and colour supplements provide us with photographs and visual information, text and lettering on a wide range of subjects. They are a rich source when it comes to making collections in a variety of forms; faces and figures to compare and use in our work, pictures of buildings to compare and to study things of architectural interest in their own locality; and pictures of animals and environments for project work on conservation (see Part 2 for more ideas).

With television and video what we need to think about as part of our art programme is the way in which visual images are presented and particularly the length of time we have to look at them. How much can we see in the few seconds given to each picture and does this affect our ability to study each other's pictures in the classroom or works of art in a gallery? In terms of art work, some programmes can provide a useful insight into composition, use of colour, and handling of images so that we can learn from them whilst remembering that they are not providing real experiences. To quote:

'If you walk over a bridge you experience it, if you drive over it's less real, if you see it on television it's less real still.'

3 Observation

3.1 CHILD DRAWING FROM OBSERVATION

AN INTRODUCTION TO OBSERVATION

Drawings made from observation are 'describing' drawings. They are made to show the appearance of things, to show how things look. But looking and seeing are two different things. We can all visit a new place and afterwards find it difficult to remember what it looked like, what colour or pattern the curtains were or what things were on the mantelpiece. That is unless they were familiar – unless they 'rang a bell' in some way. Where this happens we can remember the look of a thing because it means something to us, we have more knowledge about it than any of the other things in the room.

Working from observation gives us a chance to become familiar with a wide range of objects and things around us and to begin to build up a 'visual memory' of what things look like (figure 3.1). The scale of the work we do with children changes as they grow and in this chapter the pattern will be to look at several different types of resources and give ideas for using them, beginning with Reception and Year 1 and working through to the end of Year 6. In order not to be repetitive, age ranges will vary within each project. The ideas here are not meant to be followed step by step, but to give a general framework that you can adapt to the subjects and materials you want to use.

Because drawing is a complex activity children need help to succeed by making each step follow the last, keeping each one simple and logical. Asking them to do too much too quickly can lead to disappointment. We have to remember, too, that children in the class will work and mature at different rates. So the tasks need to be flexible, open ended and never put in such a way that a child can fail. Each activity here allows all children to work in their own way.

The following notes are general guidelines you might bear in mind for your work on observation with the children:

1 Choose objects to work from that relate to other work the children are doing.
2 Talk about and choose suitable tools and materials together.
3 Practise with the pencils, crayons or whatever you are using, making marks or blending and matching colours before beginning the actual drawing.
4 Decide how big the drawing of the object or view is going to be and encourage the children to make small, light marks to show how it fits on the paper.
5 Ask them to begin to draw lightly, looking at the whole object or view first. If they are going to be using colours ask them to work only in white, yellow or light brown first to 'place' the object on the paper and to map it out.
6 Add colour and detail after the planning.
7 Pin up or sit back from the work and get used to looking at it from a

distance. It often looks different from a metre or so away. Encourage the children to compare their drawing with the object and ask them to make any changes or additions they feel are necessary.

8 When you are discussing with the children the work they have done, look for and talk about the good things. A positive approach will give them confidence. We learn to improve by looking at right answers – not wrong ones.

9 Talk about how they might carry the work forward as a basis for an expressive or imaginative piece of work. This sort of discussion adds a further dimension to observation work.

10 Make a few notes on how the work went and any changes you might make in future using a similar resource.

In the following chapters ideas for each project are set out to give you the subject and a variety of ways of looking at it, what tools and materials you might use, some suggestions for the activities and ways of reviewing and evaluating what has happened. As you read through each project, a pattern should emerge which you can then adapt to give structure and sequence to any type of resource you want to use. There are four parts to each of the projects and they are set out as follows:

● Observing, talking and planning
● Tools, materials and equipment to use
● Activities
● Review and evaluation.

Examples are given to illustrate suitable work for **Key Stages 1 and 2** to give an outline to appropriate tasks and a sense of continuity and progression.

OURSELVES

The most obvious natural resource we have in the classroom is ourselves. Throughout **Key Stages 1 and 2** children can be encouraged to look at, draw and paint themselves and each other. Responding to this challenge in carefully structured steps will build up their confidence and the ability to tackle subjects containing figures in many different ways.

We all have access to a vast resource in terms of photographs, family albums, portraits and paintings, past and present. Looking at how people dressed and were portrayed in the past can bring an added dimension to our study of the present.

My friend – Key Stage 1
Observing, talking and planning
Paint a portrait of your best friend showing what it is you like most about them. Ask the children to look hard to see what makes their friend different from other people. Discuss with them how they might attempt to show that they like their friend in a painting. Does their friend

smile a lot, wear fashionable clothes or are they generous? How do we put these things into a picture? You might suggest they look at photographs and pictures in papers or magazines to see if they can find any clues to help them.

Materials

Use A3 buff or grey sugar paper, portrait way up (that is, with the longer side vertical) and oil pastels or ready mix paint. You can choose whether you want the children to paint the whole figure or the face. It is usually better if they do the same – it makes talking and discussing easier.

Activities

Think about the size first. Map out where the face or figure will go on the paper. It should fill the paper and to achieve this you ask them to make little marks at the top and bottom of the paper where the drawing will start and finish. They should get used to planning where things go every time they make a drawing.

Then draw in the details lightly in case any changes are required. When they are satisfied and have discussed it with you they should go on to put in details and colours.

Review and evaluation

Pin up the work and discuss how well each portrait shows the 'characteristics' they were trying to bring out. Ask the children how effectively they think they were able to describe their friend (figure 3.2). This will help them to get used to looking at and talking about their own work and that of their friends. It does not always follow that the children who are thought of as being best at drawing will be able to show in their work what it is that they liked best about their friend. Also, as it is a personal choice no one can fail. Ask the children to look carefully and see if there are things they might change next time.

3.2 'MY FRIEND'
Year 1
Tempera and crayon

Friends – Key Stage 2

Observing, talking and planning

Our friends continue to be a large part of our lives in school. Getting to know more about them and how they look is still important. At Key Stage 2 they will be able to understand, see and record more than when they were younger. They begin to look closely at the many different colours there are in hair and skin, how people look from different angles when they are sitting or standing. We can study how fabrics appear as they are draped over and around our bodies and we can search out the fine detail of pattern, texture, stitching and decoration in the clothes. All drawing takes practice but drawing ourselves and others needs repeating each year so that children build on their skills and grow more confident.

Discuss the line, shapes, form, pattern and colour in the figure. Ask the children to tell you everything they can see, then get them to look again for every detail so that they are really thinking before they start to draw. You can begin with very small sketches picking out difficult details. Look for particular folds in a shirt or the way a collar fits round a neck and do little drawings of these in rough. Try making a quick colour chart of either the colours in the hair or the skin. It is worth making separate sketches of the pattern, textures and stitching details, too, before starting to make a larger drawing.

Materials and equipment

Use cartridge or grey sugar paper for the quick sketches. For the larger drawing, use coloured sugar paper if you are using oil pastels or crayons and cartridge if the drawings are to be in pencil (HB, 2B and 4B) or black fibre tip pens. Practise using these and getting varieties of tones, very light and very strong and dark, before you start. Drawing boards will be useful so that the children can look easily from paper to figure and back.

Activities

Ask the 'model' to sit for five minutes at a time. The pose does not need to be entirely still but the model should try to keep in more or less the same position. Mark where the feet and chair, if there is one, go on the floor in case it is moved (figure 3.3). The model should take a two-minute break every five minutes to avoid becoming stiff or uncomfortable. It should be possible to keep drawing during that time, especially on details of pattern and texture that take time to make. Light and shade need to be drawn while the model is there (figure 3.4).

So, begin by mapping out the figure and choose which way up to use the paper according to the position of the model. You have to ask is the figure in this pose wider than it is high, or vice versa. After drawing the whole figure in lightly, it is best to start with the details you find most interesting – these could be the face, hair and hands or the shape made by the clothes – so that you get an overall impression of the figure before you start on the details of colour, texture and pattern (figure 3.5).

3.3   CHILDREN DRAWING FROM A MODEL
Year 6

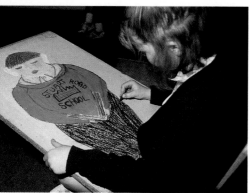

3.4   CHILD WORKING ON A DRAWING
Year 6
Oil pastel

3.5 'MY FRIEND'
Year 4
Tempera

3.6 DRAWING FROM A MODEL
Year 5
Pencil

If the drawings take more than one session to complete, you will have the marks you made to pose the model again and the drawings to help (figure 3.6).

Review and evaluation

Pin up the work and discuss the good points of each drawing. Even professional artists find it difficult to get a likeness because we all see something different in people, especially our friends, so this should not be one of the criteria used in evaluating the work. The important aspects of the drawing are how well the overall pose has been achieved, how accurately the colours have been matched and how closely the patterns and textures were observed. People are probably more complicated and difficult to draw than most other things so we should understand that it takes patience and lots of practice. It is important to applaud progress and success.

People who visit our school – Key Stage 1

Observing, talking and planning

This activity is particularly suitable for young children as it helps them to get to know more about their school and the people they might see from time to time. You could ask one of the visitors if they would be kind enough to sit for the children. This can be quite informal. All they need do is to spend five minutes with you whilst the children make a drawing. At this age children tend to want to work quickly and the ¨aintings can be finished from memory, if necessary. You could also ask your visitor to say a little about what brings them to the school, what they will be doing and why and something about their job, if that is appropriate. Suggest to the children that they look carefully at the clothes the visitor is wearing.

Materials

Use A3 coloured sugar paper, portrait way up, and ready mix, powder paints, or wax crayons.

Activities

Follow the routine of mapping out where the figure should go and see that it fills the paper. Suggest how they might make a suitable colour to match the skin if you feel that this would help them to be satisfied with the results (see figures 3.7 and 3.8).

Review and evaluation

Pin up the work and ask your visitor to call back, if possible, to see it so that the children can talk about the things they felt were important to them and what they chose to put into their pictures.

People who visit our school – Key Stage 2, Years 3 and 4

You will now be able to look in more detail at this subject.

Observing, talking and planning

Ask your visitor to talk about him/herself, to describe the job they do and the place where they do it – putting it into context is important at this age. Give the children the opportunity to ask questions.

Materials

Use A3 cartridge paper, portrait way up, and pencil or biro. The children should again be encouraged to map out very lightly where the figure will go. Remind them that they cannot change their minds when using biro and it is better not to have to use a rubber with pencil. Very light marks can be drawn over and changed if needed.

Activities

Make drawings to show what sort of person you are looking at, based on what you know about him/her from listening to what they had to say about their job. Ask them to look for as much detail as they can find. Then, if you wish, they can add their own impression of the sort of place the visitor works (see figure 3.9).

Review and evaluation

Spread out the work and discuss it with the children. Ask them if they think they have seen and responded to different things about their visitor and how these are portrayed in their drawing. Can we learn from this? If there is an opportunity to share the drawings with the visitor, perhaps he/she may like to make some comments too.

3.7 SCHOOL DOCTOR
Year 1
Tempera

3.8 SCHOOL NURSE
Year 1
Tempera

3.9 SCHOOL TRAFFIC WARDEN
Year 2
Pencil

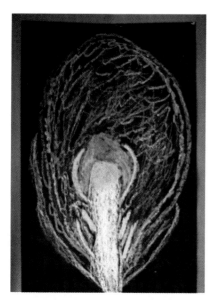

**3.10 DRAWING OF A SPROUT
CUT IN HALF**
Year 5
Oil pastel

**3.11 DRAWING OF A SPROUT
CUT IN HALF**
Year 5
Oil pastel

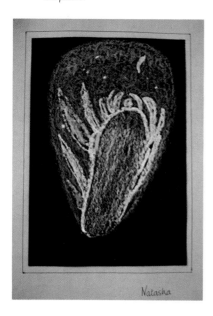

THE NATURAL WORLD

We need to give children the opportunity to become familiar with natural things, to know where they come from and how they come to be. We also need to encourage children to look again at their environment and to focus on things which they may take for granted, know exist but do not understand or appreciate.

Plants

The world is full of plants that many of us take for granted. In looking at them afresh we can learn about how they grow, mature, produce seeds and regenerate themselves. Flowers, fruit, vegetables, shrubs, trees and leaves – an enormous variety, from blades of grass to fields of corn – or we can concentrate on garden produce or food and flowers found in the supermarket.

With **Key Stage 1**, looking, talking and drawing will help to focus attention on all these familiar things. Then, as the children get older and move into **Key Stage 2**, they will be able to respond in more detail and with a growing awareness. You can adapt the sections that follow to suit the age of your children in the way which is outlined in the section on drawing people.

Humble and ordinary things can be as equally exciting as the unfamiliar if we see them from a different perspective. Expensive vegetables, like green and red sweet peppers, are often used for drawing but sprouts can be just as interesting at a fraction of the cost.

Sprouts
Observing, talking and planning

Work in pairs, one sprout to each pair of children. Study the whole sprout carefully. Discuss together the way that the leaves overlap, talk about the way the colours change and make a small drawing, looking particularly at the shape. Then cut the sprout in half, top to stem. Each child will then have their own half to study, a mirror image of the other. As all natural things have grown individually, each sprout is unique and no two are exactly the same, so the drawings will be different. Talk about the sprout. Look at the solid, central 'trunk' which is similar in some ways to a tree trunk, or a single leaf. At the base, the leaves begin to grow strongly, then at the top they are still emerging and are full of crinkles. If you can get a sprout plant, or a picture of one, it will help to explain how they grow out of each leaf joint.

Materials

Use A3 black sugar paper, portrait way up, and oil pastels. These materials will make it easy to show the shape and colour of the sprout.

Activities

Draw the outside balloon-like shape in white pastel first, then the stalk or core. Mark in where each leaf grows out of the stalk or stem, working up as the leaves grow and watching carefully where the leaves change from being straight to crinkly. Next, talk about the colours and make them, starting with the light creamy-white colours and working through yellow to a variety of greens. Finally, use the colours you have made to colour in the drawing (figures 3.10 and 3.11).

Review and evaluation

Spread out the work and talk about how each one looks different. Did the children appreciate that each spout was unique and that cut in half they form a mirror image? Were they satisfied that they had matched the colours accurately? Were they able to estimate how many sprouts can grow on a single plant?

Flowers and flowering plants – Key Stage 2
Observing, talking and planning

The difference between garden and wild flowers is an interesting one. It is fascinating to study how our cultivated varieties have been developed and bred from their wild ancestors. You could try to identify one or two flowers which have their origins in wild plants you know. In recent years it has become possible to buy wild flower seeds at garden centres and we are being encouraged to plant them in order to create wild gardens in an effort to conserve, support and provide for birds, animals and insects.

Foxgloves are relatively common. They begin to grow in April and will flower in June and July in most parts of this country. They are quite complicated in that each flower begins to grow evenly spaced around the stem, but as they get taller the flower heads move round all on to the same side (see figure 3.12). It might be interesting to try to find out why. Is it so that they face the sun or because they often grow on banks and face towards the light? The answer may lie in your Science lessons.

Holly, ivy, brambles and evergreens are also familiar and even grow on walls and in open spaces in our cities (figures 3.13 and 3.14).

3.12 FOXGLOVES
Year 1/2
Tempera

3.13 HOLLY
Year 5
Watercolour

3.14 BLACKBERRIES
Year 6
Pencil

3.15 HEDGEROW
Year 6
Watercolour

Cutting or picking wild plants is not allowed so you may need to take sketchbooks and draw them where they are growing unless you have them in your own garden or permission to collect a few samples. Hedgerows offer the richest source of weeds and wild flowers and the opportunity to draw several plants growing together rather than individual specimens (figure 3.15).

Houseplants are easily available and a worthwhile, long lasting and renewable resource. They offer us a whole cycle from growing to flowering and then the flowers, hopefully not the plant, dying. They also tend to have a wide variety of differently shaped and coloured leaves and flowers that we can contrast with each other.

Materials
Use coloured sugar paper to fit the size of the flower or plant or larger to allow room to show the detail, and pastels or cartridge paper if you are using coloured pencils.

Activities
Map out the shape of the plant to fill the paper and draw it lightly. Begin with the lightest colour and add the darker ones as you work. Look particularly at the shapes, patterns and structure in the plant (figure 3.16). Take particular care to see that the leaves or flowers at the back are drawn in slightly paler colours than those at the front or nearest to you so that they will appear to be further away in the drawing.

Review and evaluation
Pin up the work and display it with the flowers or plants if you have room. Ask the children to tell you of any new things they learnt about the plant they were drawing and look at the way other artists have drawn and painted flowers, fruit and plants.

3.16 CYCLAMEN
Year 3
Oil pastel

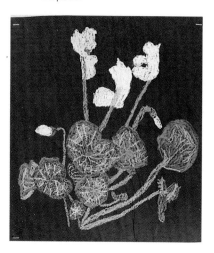

THE MADE WORLD

All around us we can find familiar, intriguing and interesting everyday objects that we tend to take for granted. How detailed are they? How were they made? The way we might begin to work with made objects will follow more or less the same pattern. Ask the children what they know about it. Get them to share their knowledge first so you can go on to explore together as much as you can find about it. It will suffice, here, to look at two groups of made objects, one in each Key Stage, because there are many similarities in the ways of looking, choosing materials and making the drawing as in those of the natural world.

Familiar things – Key Stage 1
Small children love to look at familiar things and by drawing them will get to know them better and find out more about them. Keep the scale small, so that the children are not overwhelmed by complexities. The

3.17 TEAPOT AND DRAWINGS
Year 1
Crayon

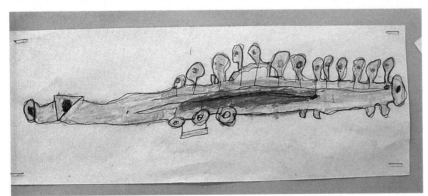

3.18 DRAWINGS OF TEAPOTS
Year 1
Crayon

3.19 CLARINET
Year 2
Pencil and crayon

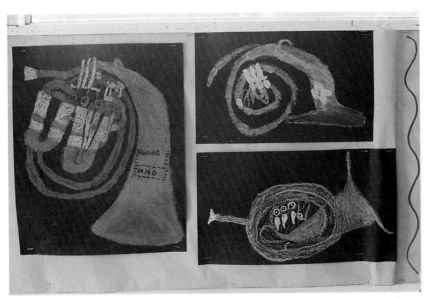

3.20 FRENCH HORN
Year 2
Oil pastel

more they enjoy the things and feel at home with them the more they will gain from drawing and painting them. Things that are in everyday use like teapots (figures 3.17 and 3.18) and the instruments they see being used in school (figures 3.19 and 3.20) make ideal subjects for observation work.

You should ask the children to look and draw these in just the same way as in the example illustrated below which focuses on bears. Children love to collect and bring in their teddy bears because they hold such a strong place in their affections (figure 3.21). In Reception you can simply talk and paint (figure 3.22). Years 1 and 2 will be able to take it further and a sequence of work will best help them to make informed drawings.

Observing, talking and planning

Begin by looking at two teddies and comparing them. Make small, quick sketches to show how they are different.

Materials

For this use pencils and cartridge paper. Then decide on the paper and materials you will use for the coloured picture, probably crayons or

3.21 CLASSROOM COLLECTION OF TEDDY BEARS

3.22 TEDDY
Reception
Tempera

pastels would make it easiest and grey or buff sugar paper (about A3) so that the teddy just about fills the paper. If you hold the teddy in front of the paper it will make it easy to see how big the drawing ought to be.

Activities

Practise making the colours first; then draw the teddy using white or a pale colour first; add the colours and give special attention to the pattern and texture of the fur (figures 3.23 and 3.24).

Review and evaluation

Pin up the work and display the teddy bears with it (figure 3.25). Talk about what you enjoyed most about the drawing and what other toys, dolls or playthings it might be nice to draw next.

3.25 TEDDY
Year 1/2
Oil pastel

3.23 TEDDY
Year 2
Pencil, oil pastel

3.24 TEDDY
Year 2
Oil pastel

Christopher.

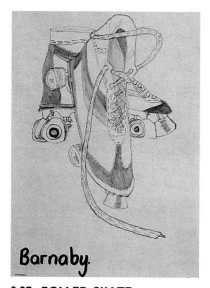

3.26 ROLLER SKATES
Year 6
Pencil

Barnaby.

3.27 ROLLER SKATE
Year 6
Pencil

Familiar things – Key Stage 2

With this age group you need to move on to more complex objects which challenge the children to look very closely. They need to be intrigued and curious about the objects and to have a real reason for looking. Try to choose things which already have meaning for them – objects which relate to other work that they may be doing. In figures 3.26 and 3.27 we can see how fascinated they have been with some roller skates that children in the class were becoming proficient in using. Still on the theme of wheels a teacher had asked the schools' police liaison officer if he would be kind enough to let them draw his colleague's official motorcycle (figures 3.28 and 3.29). The joy of having this machine in the playground was that the officer could not turn the radio off in case he was needed urgently. So the dialogue continued throughout the time the children were drawing, with the ever present thought that the officer might be called away at any moment. Thus the drawings needed to be made as quickly as possible.

If you are going to use things in other areas of interest, you might choose to look at current projects; for example, a language-based topic on the Second World War. *Carrie's War* is a book that is frequently used in fiction-based projects to give some focus and meaning to this period. It provides a wonderful opportunity to ask parents and grandparents to lend things they have kept since those times. In this example, we look at the way a gas mask was used to try to make it real for the children.

This example can equally well apply to other objects that have meaning for the children.

Observing, talking and planning

Everyone needs to examine the gas mask before they begin to draw. They need to talk about why they think these forms of protection were necessary, who would have worn them and what sort of threat there was to the way of life of people in another country. You might feel it

3.28 POLICE MOTORCYCLE
Year 6
Pencil

appropriate to draw parallels with things that are happening in the present day.

Then you could begin to look at the object in some detail. How are the straps fastened around the back of the head? How many different materials is it made from and how does the stitching hold it all together? The actual relic was brought in by one child's grandfather and he talked about how it felt to wear it, about the bombing raids, the air-raid shelters and the fear that they felt with all the noise, destruction and desolation. The children took turns at wearing the mask to see how difficult it was to breathe through the fine metal mesh.

Materials and equipment

Use A3 cartridge paper, portrait way up, and pencils or biros. A fine point will be necessary in order to be able to show the detail in the drawings. Drawing boards will be useful.

Activities

Begin by asking one child to wear the mask and to sit for the others, or, if you can organise it, so that only half of the children do their drawings at a time so they can comfortably see the mask from the front. When drawing from observation like this the children will need to look again and again because the shapes are so complex. It will help them if they have drawing boards that they can rest against the edge of the table, so that their drawing paper is at an angle and it is easier to look up and down again and again. Practise making the patterns created by the mesh and the stitching first, then map out the size of the head and the gas mask in light marks. After this, ask the children to look again to see which areas are light and which are heavy and dark. Where are the patterns and where is it plain? (see figures 3.30 and 3.31). Generally they will only flounder if left too long without being reminded to take another look.

**3.30 BOY WEARING A
SECOND WORLD WAR
GAS MASK**
Year 5
Pencil

**3.31 BOY WEARING A
SECOND WORLD WAR
GAS MASK**
Year 5
Pencil

3.32 OUR SCHOOL BUS
Year 1
Tempera

Review and evaluation
Did the children appreciate why gas masks were issued to everyone and why they had to practise wearing them? Could you or they find any present day equivalent that perhaps had been seen in the newspapers or on television news where governments had enforced action because of a threat? Questions like these need to be a part of any review of work to reinforce its relevance to our own lives today.

Our environment – Key Stage 1

Studying the surroundings of your school, looking at the playground, houses, streets, shops, churches and vehicles that we take for granted as part of the everyday world we might benefit from getting closer and recording some of the things we see. The things which will tend to mean most to younger children are those which they use and know most about. They sometimes travel on buses (figures 3.32 and 3.33) and often see building work going on around them. As you will appreciate in this Key Stage children are quite happy to draw from memory, but it is important to introduce working from observation so that the children get used to looking at real things in the environment as well as in their classroom.

Observing, talking and planning
If you have any building or construction work going on in your area, ask the children to look at the way the bulldozers work and how they move great mounds of rubble. Suggest that this is a way of recording the changes that are taking place.

Materials
Use ready mixed paint and a firm sugar paper that won't buckle with water.

Activities

Ask the children to paint a picture of the playground while the JCBs are working (figure 3.34) and what the playground looks like when they have finished (figure 3.35).

Review and evaluation

Pin up the paintings and discuss how different the playground looks now. Ask the children if they can remember what it looked like before the bulldozers moved in. This will apply equally well if you use a local building site or housing estate.

3.33 BUS WITH THE SUN SHINING
Year I
Tempera

3.34 EXCAVATORS IN OUR PLAYGROUND
Reception/Year I
Tempera

3.35 OUR PLAYGROUND
Year I
Tempera

Our environment – Key Stage 2

We continue, here, to narrow the focus and look in greater detail at our surroundings. In this example we take one aspect of the local church, making careful observed drawings and bringing them back to develop into paintings. All making should be founded on close observation and this theme is dealt with more fully in Part 2 'Making in Art'.

Observing, talking and planning

When the children are looking at your local church, in connection with a project on history or an environmental study, you could take them there to make drawings of specific areas to compare various features. Doors, windows, the font, pulpit, altar and all the columns and carvings are among our greatest local treasures. Whether it is a new building designed by a living architect or hundreds of years old, it is bound to offer a rich resource for observation work.

3.36 SKETCH OF A CHURCH DOORWAY
Year 5/6
Pencil

3.37 PAINTING OF THE CHURCH DOORWAY, MADE FROM THE SKETCH
Year 5/6
Watercolour

Materials and equipment

Take small drawing boards with A3 paper if this is possible or clipboards with A4 cartridge paper and pencils and graphite sticks for drawing. Back in the classroom you could use coloured inks, watercolours or tempera for making the paintings.

Activities

At the site make drawings which show the lines, tones and distance and light and shade. It is important to show the background, middle distance and foreground clearly by drawing them in paler tones for the distance and stronger ones for things that are close. In the classroom when you make the paintings remember to do the same; keep the colours and tones light in the distance and bright, strong and clear in the foreground.

Review and evaluation

Pin up the work, sketches, working drawings and finished work together (figures 3.36 to 3.39). If you were able to organise groups of children to record different parts of the church, there should be a comprehensive picture of the type of architecture and the particular way that the church was built. Remember these buildings are not like those in the high street where you might expect to see the same frontage and layout whichever town or city it is in. Your church is a unique building, special to its place and the community it serves.

3.38 SKETCH OF THE CHURCH INTERIOR
Year 5/6
Pencil

3.39 PAINTING OF THE CHURCH INTERIOR, MADE FROM THE SKETCH
Year 5/6
Watercolour

4 Investigative drawing

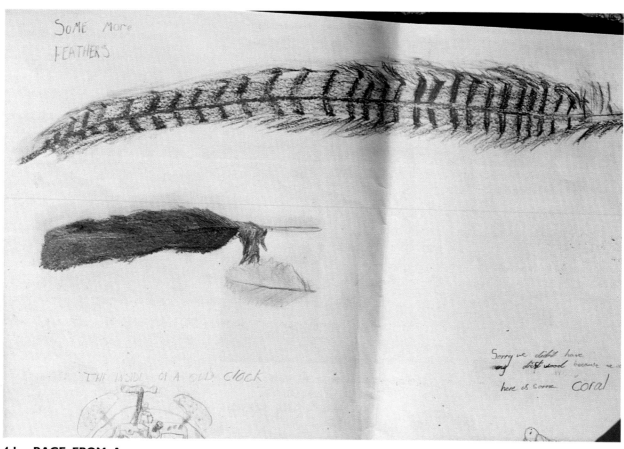

**4.1 PAGE FROM A
SKETCHBOOK**
Year 5
Pencil and crayon

INTRODUCTION

To some extent all drawing is an investigation into what things look like, what they are made of and how they grow or work. It is by drawing, discussing and looking that we learn about things, decide what materials best suit describing and recording each object and learn how to increase our understanding of the tools and materials that are available to us.

Study skills are taught so that children can learn to carry out research for themselves, analyse their findings and use their knowledge to express and communicate their ideas. This process of gathering information is fundamental. In all forms of art, craft and design, research and investigation become more important as children get older providing them with data on which to base their work. Knowing which tools and materials to use with different resources is also important if tasks are to be manageable; then they can actively help the children to succeed.

The investigative skills which are so important are:

● note taking, sketching and writing
● collecting, ordering and classifying information
● use of time spent on research
● matching materials to resources
● use of different focusing devices.

Note taking, sketching and writing

In **Key Stage 1** you should include introducing a sketchbook in its simplest form. This could consist of, perhaps, four or six sheets of A3 or A4 paper in different colours to make it interesting – folded and stapled. Thus each child has a place to record events and begins to learn how to make notes on things of interest that they see. It is somewhere to build up lists of new words and begin to introduce an art vocabulary that they can then use to enhance their ability to describe things and processes.

In **Key Stage 2** either home-made or simple, inexpensive sketchbooks give the children a chance to build up their own resource ideas and make a series of drawings and notes on things of current interest (figure 4.1). They are also important as ways of remembering things seen and recorded in the past which may be referred to later on. Keeping a record provides more than evidence of visual information: it builds a habit of looking and recording which in its turn helps children to become more discriminating.

Collecting, ordering and classifying information

Here we recognise the importance of getting children to look at their environment and begin to make connections between objects, noticing similarities and differences (figure 4.2). Patterns of growth or manufacture can be recognised and children can become aware of families of objects in the way that they use Venn diagrams in Maths. Taking shells as an example, the children could sort them into groups by shape (like round, conical, tubular or flat), into different colours or by patterns

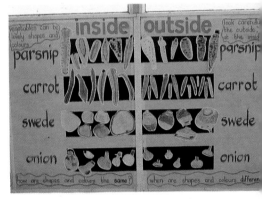

4.2 VEGETABLES
Year 2
Oil pastels
A collection of vegetables drawn to compare what they look like inside and outside.

4.3   COLLECTION OF SHELLS

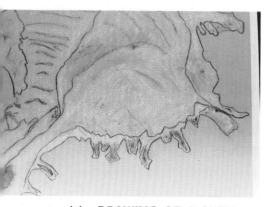

4.4   DRAWING OF A SHELL
Year 6
Crayon and chalks

(ridged and smooth). Then if they appreciate that they are all homes for some type of sea creature they could add the different sorts of places that they live (see figures 4.3 and 4.4). As with all their drawing and recording, the greater the understanding the more the children will be able to put into their work.

Use of time spent on research

Using time well is a constructive way of keeping work moving forwards and will avoid lingering too long on an individual piece, allowing interest to flag. The National Curriculum working party, in their report *Art for ages 5 to 14*, found that an average of two hours a week was spent on art at **Key Stage 1** and one hour forty minutes in **Key Stage 2**. In order to make maximum use of this time you should think in terms of talking about and discussing which tools and materials to use with the resources you have chosen as part of the research. Collect supporting objects, pictures and information and planning the order of events for when you begin the work. Apart from the security this provides, it means that every child understands what is happening and is actively involved for the whole time. It is also important to vary the types of project. For example, extended ones which follow a series of explorations and require a lot of background research, contrasted with short ones, which highlight different aspects of Art and Design in conjunction with particular resources and for which reference material from sketchbooks will furnish all the necessary information.

Matching materials to resources

This illustrates ways of introducing children to the wide variety of tools and materials available to us. The children need to spend long enough exploring the possibilities of each one to get a thorough understanding of the range of uses it may have. They also need to know which ones may be most appropriate to use with different resources. To take an obvious example, if the children are going to draw daffodils they should be encouraged to use dark paper, cut to the size of the flower and stem (about 12 × 30 cm), and a range of white, yellow and green oil pastels. Imagine how much more difficult the task would be if they had to work with pencils on rectangular white paper and had to draw coloured objects in black on a white background. Alternatively, if they are working on something which has very fine detail, like a tree with intricate twigs and branches or the shell of a tortoise with a detailed pattern, then pencil would be entirely appropriate.

Charcoal and chalk work well together and offer a good way of drawing from black, grey and white resources like pebbles, feathers or metal (see figures 4.5 and 4.6). The teaching point here is that the children should draw with the chalk first. They will soon appreciate that it is easier to change the drawing if they want to if it is in white rather than black. Adding the charcoal to the chalk makes a better range of greys. (Try this out and see if you agree!)

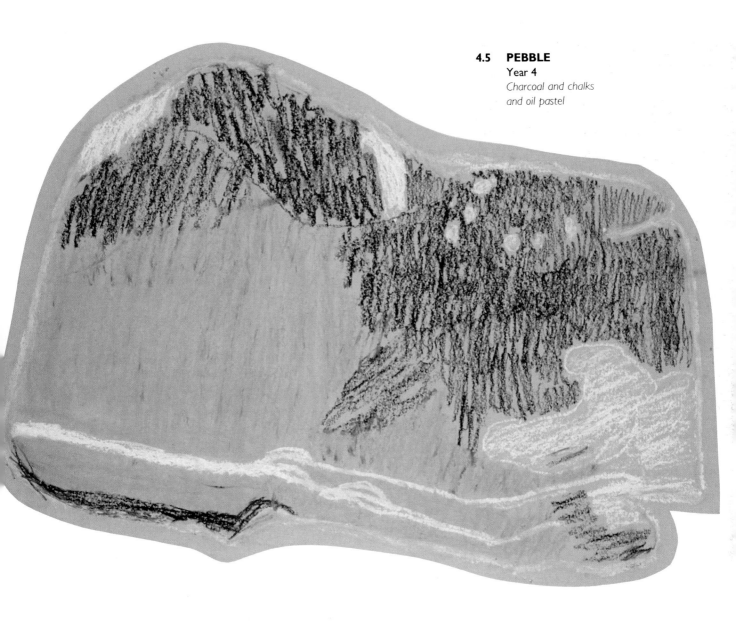

4.5 PEBBLE
Year 4
*Charcoal and chalks
and oil pastel*

4.6 DRAWING OF A FEATHER
Year 6
Charcoal and chalk

Use of different focusing devices

There are a wide range of focusing devices available to us including viewfinders which we make for ourselves, magnifying glasses, mirrors and reflective surfaces. Viewfinders are usually made out of card – simple rectangular, square or even keyhole-shaped holes in the centre of a piece of black card. They are used to isolate the part of an object or view you want to draw so that you only see what you want to look at, in a frame, with no additional information. For instance, if you wanted the children to draw landscapes the viewfinders could be lightly stuck on to the window so that they could be sure of seeing the same view each time. An extension of this, in order to see exactly the same view, is to use a small, square or rectangular box, stuck to the glass – so it is like looking down a telescope. This makes it easier to focus directly on the part of the landscape you want to draw or paint.

Magnifying glasses help us to see fine details and we use them to draw from small objects in the same way in Art that we record the appearance of things for Science. It may help, too, if you give the children round paper to work on so that they can match what they see through the magnifying glass to the shape of the paper.

Mirrors in which we can see ourselves and other things from unusual angles, and in reverse, are useful ways of seeing something new. They can also be used as a tool to focus attention on just what is reflected, like a viewfinder, cutting out all extraneous information.

Reflective surfaces include any shiny objects such as old kettles, car hub caps, flattened pieces of tin, windows, puddles and silver backed gift wrapping paper. All of which help children to draw what they see reflected in them with a sense of fascination, not self-consciousness.

Investigation and research give children the means by which they can find out how to plan their own projects. This is introduced as a gradual process where they should take on more of the decisions which have to be made about how to proceed with their work. In the early years you need to keep asking questions about the objects the children are looking at so that they will begin to ask those questions for themselves as a part of their investigation, providing knowledge on which to base their work.

Discussion during and after each piece of work is equally important. It provides an opportunity to consider how well the tools and materials suited the subject matter and to look at how much progress has been made in handling them. As each school term passes you should plan to increase the amount of information the children collect and there should be more discussion about the most suitable materials to use.

Investigation and research will help children to find out new things about the world and they should also be learning to understand which tools and materials will best help to record them. We need to look at examples of how to get the balance right in this combination of looking, finding out and making.

INVESTIGATING THE NATURAL WORLD

The Programmes of Study call for recording from direct observation of the natural world. We can look here at some of the means we might employ to structure the children's investigation so that each new piece of work builds on previous knowledge, growing out of things they already know and can do. Beginning with investigation appropriate to Reception and Year 1, this section will outline the way the enquiry might develop through to Year 6. We will look, in turn, at finding out about colour, growth patterns, shape, composition and the effects of light on a form.

All natural things have a life cycle and if we know what plants look like in different stages of their lives it will help us to make better drawings and to record their appearance with greater understanding. Investigating may involve gathering some information from the living plant, but also from books and pictures, to support our understanding where it is not possible to see at first hand the actual thing. For example, we are all familiar with coffee beans but many of us are only likely to see the plant they grow on in a hothouse; so photographs or good illustrations will be the only way to research the growth cycle.

In figure 4.7 the children looked at the colours in a bunch of flowers. Using powder colours they selected a range of reds and blues to mix together to match the colours they could see in the flowers. Their paintings were made directly from these colours.

Figures 4.8 and 4.9 use pencil and watercolour to give us information about trees. In the first, a sketchbook has been used to write about the

4.7 RED FLOWERS
Year 1
Powder colour

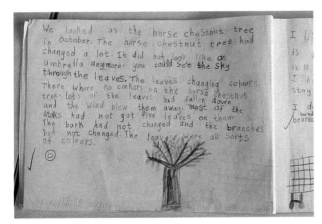

4.8 HORSE CHESTNUT
Year 1
Pencil and crayon

4.9 HORSE CHESTNUTS
Year 2
Pencil and crayon

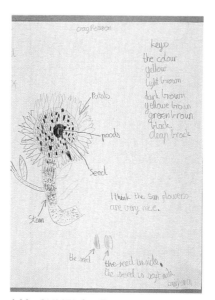

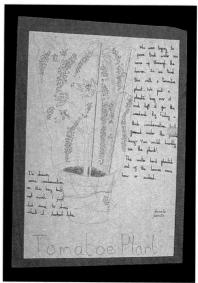

4.10   RED CABBAGES
Year 1
Oil pastels

4.11   SUNFLOWER
Year 4
Pencil
A drawing made to show and
explain its various parts.

4.12   TOMATO PLANT
Year 6
Pencil
A drawing made to show how
plants give off water vapour.

growth and illustrate the development of a horse chestnut tree. The second shows coloured drawings of the way horse chestnut twigs open. They were drawn every other day for two weeks as they grew.

Using a dry colour medium like oil pastels enables a whole class to work together to investigate the intricate lines and colour of vegetables, like the red cabbage in figure 4.10. It can be cut into sections so that each group of three or four children has its own slice to study. The brilliance of colour that can be produced from these pastels make it relatively easy for the children to record directly what they see.

Pencils used on white paper are an excellent way of describing a variety of resources. Objects with fine lines and intricate details, like spiders sitting on webs or drops of water running down the window pane, may need written notes to explain the details. Pencils are good for this, unlike pastels, chalks or paints. Sunflowers are common and often grown in the school grounds as part of other studies. They have a most complicated arrangement of seeds which is composed of a series of interrelated spirals, each one like the 'Nautilus' curve which expands out from the centre in an ever widening curve. Once the pattern is understood, making a drawing becomes far less complicated. This pattern is shared with many forms in nature; for example, fir cones, some shells and many cactus plants. For those with a mathematical curiosity this is based on the 'Fibonacci' series of numbers. Investigative drawings to show how a sunflower grows will probably need written notes as well (figure 4.11), so pencils will be the best choice here.

In a similar way, drawings made to record scientific experiments will need to show the detailed result. In this case, the aim was to record

what happened when a plant was put into a plastic bag over night (figure 4.12). The comment made on this drawing records a degree of selection:

> 'I only drew some of the water bubbles otherwise it would have been difficult to see the tomato plant.'

Pencil is also an appropriate choice to show the effect of light on an object; in the case of figure 4.13 on some apples. The children need to practise with a range of pencils, from HB to 4B or 6B first to know how many greys they can make between the lightest and darkest shades. Looking at any round, shiny forms you can see where the light is changing the appearance of the object.

For drawings which require fine lines and some colour to give all the information, pencils and water colour together make a good combination. These are coloured drawings rather than paintings and are there specifically to tell us about how things are made or grow. Written notes are important here too (figure 4.14). Useful reference for this type of work can be found in books by Marjorie Blamey and in nineteenth century botanical prints.

LOOKING AT OURSELVES

Finding out how things really look is a gradual process helped on by investigating and recording our impressions. In **Key Stage 1**, children are still drawing as much what they know as what they see. Tables are drawn as square or rectangular until the child begins to ask questions about how to make them look more real. At this point you should introduce familiar things in contexts which make it easy to see the

4.13 APPLES
Year 5
Pencil
A drawing made to show the effect of light on a shiny surface.

4.14 DAFFODILS
Year 6
Pencil and watercolour
Drawing and notes made to explain what a daffodil looks like.

**4.15   CHILDREN STANDING IN
A CIRCLE**
Year 2
Pencil

**4.16   CHILDREN STANDING IN
A CIRCLE**
Year 2
Pencil

**4.18   USING A MIRROR TO
DRAW A SELF-PORTRAIT**

4.17   SELF-PORTRAIT
Year 3
Pencil and felt tip pen
A drawing made to explain details
about myself.

difference between 'aerial' views and more realistic viewpoints. For example, get some of the children to stand in a circle and take it in turns to see what they look like (figures 4.15 and 4.16). Pencils or fibre tip pens will be the best choice here so that things seen one behind the other can be described clearly. Children come to this change in perception in their own time but exercises like this will give you the opportunity to see where they are in their development and give them appropriate tasks.

Also in this Key Stage in their Science lessons children will be studying 'Me and my body', so it is a good time to make drawings explaining things about ourselves (figure 4.17) and to introduce looking at works of art showing people in all kinds of settings. Making drawings of parts of ourselves using mirrors means that we can get to know more about how we look from different points of view (figure 4.18).

In **Key Stage 2** , using other focusing devices adds interest and avoids any feelings of self-consciousness. As before, using chalk and charcoal will probably work best when looking at reflections in metal surfaces and grey paper provides the best ground to use (see figures 4.19 to 4.21).

You can further extend the idea of looking at parts of faces using mirrors by asking the children to make comparisons between themselves and their friends. These 'identikit' type drawings can be made using pencils to show the detail (figure 4.22). Following the same theme, you could ask the children to make a drawing of themselves from an unusual point of view using mirrors. If they hold the mirror under their chin or by their ear (figures 4.23 and 4.24), the reflection they see is distorted.

4.19 USING A HUB CAP TO DRAW A DISTORTED SELF-PORTRAIT

4.20 SELF-PORTRAIT
Year 6
Charcoal and chalk
Using the back of an old spoon to draw a distorted self-portrait.

4.21 USING A FLATTENED PIECE OF TIN TO DRAW A DISTORTED SELF-PORTRAIT

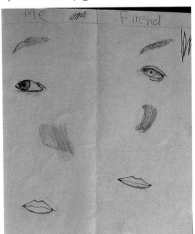

4.22 COMPARING FEATURES WITH A FRIEND
Year 5/6
Pencil

4.23 MY REFLECTION IN A MIRROR HELD BY MY EAR
Year 6
Pencil

4.24 MY REFLECTION IN A MIRROR HELD NEARLY UNDER MY CHIN
Year 6
Pencil

INVESTIGATING THE MADE WORLD

Having looked at ways of matching materials to suit the type of work being undertaken, we can concentrate here on the types of research which will help children to get to know how to handle more complex shapes and structures. They need to be given a clear purpose and reason to make their investigations. Children in **Key Stage I** benefit from any experiences which will develop their vocabulary. Discussing how things are made and put together should offer rich opportunities. The qualities which make nets so interesting are their patterns and the way they are distorted by movement (figures 4.25 and 4.26). In addition to fishing nets, there are a tremendous number of different types of wire and plastic netting made for use in the garden. These have many different sizes and shapes of mesh and in your discussion about them you could talk about the purposes for which nets are used. Extremely fine drift nets used to capture birds for ringing can be contrasted with those that are attached to cranes for lifting heavy cargo on to ships in port. You could encourage the children to make a collection of actual nets and illustrations of them being used for a variety of purposes. They could even go on to design their own nets for some special need they have identified.

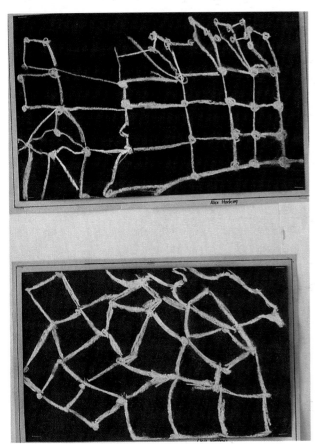

4.26 FISHING NETS
Year 2
Oil pastel and fibre tip pen

4.25 FISHING NETS
Year 2
Oil pastel

Simple things in everyday use make good resources for investigating colour and design. Woven and knitted fabrics seen through a magnifying glass are challenging to draw and enrich our understanding of the way things are made (figure 4.27). Wrapping papers, packaging and wallpapers are readily available and, as with the nets, offer opportunities for all kinds of research and design (figure 4.28).

4.27 PATTERN
Year 2
Pencil, crayon and felt tip pen

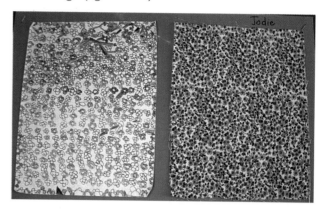

4.28 PATTERN
Year 2
Felt tip pens
Drawing on the left made to show
the colours and pattern on the
piece of fabric.

In **Key Stage 2**, more use can be made of sketchbooks to record visual and written information, especially from things seen in the environment or at home. Again you can stress that it is the reason for making the drawing that is important. We need to look specifically at how things are made or how they work (figures 4.29 and 4.30). It may be necessary to make a series of drawings to explain more complex things or to make several drawings of them from different points of view. It can be challenging and interesting to turn small things on their side or upside down so that they are seen from an unfamiliar angle. It sometimes makes for a more informative drawing too.

4.29 VALVE AND TRANSISTORS
Year 5
Pencil

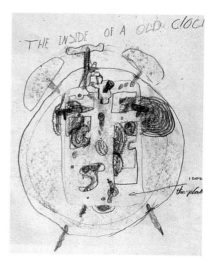

4.30 ALARM CLOCK
Year 5
Pencil and crayon

Your choice of resources to use should be based on things of current interest to the children and link with projects or topics they are studying. In Technology, for instance, a familiar topic is fastenings – so bolts, latches, laces, zips and buckles can make fascinating objects to draw.

Systems which carry out operations may also be described in drawings. Within the school you are likely to have access to a variety of mechanical devices, including vacuum cleaners (figure 4.31), film and slide projectors and screens all of which change their appearance when they are working to how they look when they are switched off. Bicycles have many working parts and offer opportunities to investigate how different parts work (figures 4.32 and 4.33).

4.31 VACUUM CLEANERS
Year 6
Charcoal

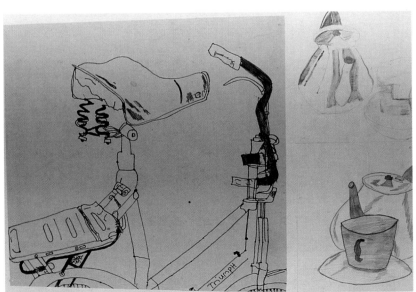

4.32 MOTORBIKE HANDLEBARS
Year 4
Pencil
Drawing to show how the handlebars worked.

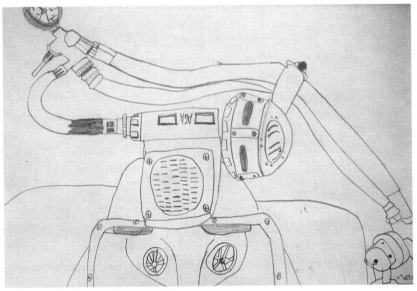

4.33 BICYCLE
Year 5
Pencil
Drawing made to show how the saddle was fixed.

INVESTIGATING OUR ENVIRONMENT

Looking at the landscape offers scope to use sketchbooks again. There are many ways of investigating the environment, finding and recording information about specific aspects of your locality by comparing appearances and materials. So many questions can be asked about buildings. For example, what are they made of and how were they built? Do you live in an area where the local stone is used or are the houses built of brick and timber? How have the doors and window frames been set into the walls? What shape is the roof and how is it covered?

In order to investigate this complicated subject you will need a clear strategy which focuses on one particular aspect. You will need to take the children out into the locality so that they can make sketches of the buildings from the point of view you and they have chosen. As an addition to their drawings the children could also make a collection of pictures from papers and magazines on the same topic and use them to support their enquiry.

The focus for these visits can range from looking at and comparing the windows, doors or other features common to houses, shops and public buildings. Depending on the area, your researches might focus on the types of lettering on shop fronts, or on the design of lampposts or street names. The focus for the drawings might equally well be to identify the history of the area, to use later for making a painting about the place you live in or to make a map of where your school is in relation to the rest of the community (figure 4.34).

Maps can be made for other purposes in that they may be made to find out how best to organise, plan or record an area (figure 4.35). The ability to draw a helpful and reasonably accurate map of how to get from one place to another is a skill which will be of lasting value.

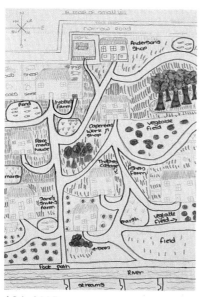

4.34 MAP
Year 6
Felt tip pens

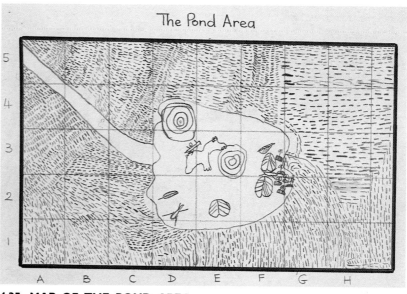

4.35 MAP OF THE POND AREA
Year 5
Pencil

AN ENVIRONMENTAL RESEARCH PROJECT

This study combines several different areas of research. The initial task was to identify and compare all the various types and patterns of stained glass in the locality (figures 4.36 and 4.37). Sketches were made in some detail and notes written to record the size of windows and thickness and colour of the glass. The second visit made was to the hedgerow surrounding the school to make drawings of plants with leaves and berries. Then using the shapes and proportions of one of the windows they had sketched, the children cut out their own frames and used them to isolate a part of their plant study that they thought would make the best and most interesting design (figure 4.38). The final drawings were made first to fit the frames and then watercolours used to complete them (figures 4.39 and 4.40).

This project was spread over several lessons and gave the children time to make careful sketches and then modify and refine them into polished and considered pieces of work. In any drawing or painting you cannot give all the information that is there so children need to learn how to select which aspects to focus on. Understanding the role of investigation and research will help them to be confident in making choices and give them a framework on which to base future projects.

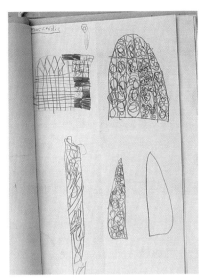

4.37 WINDOW DESIGNS
Year 2
Biro

4.36 WINDOW SHAPES
Year 2
Felt tip pens

4.38 WINDOW DESIGN RESEARCH – HEDGEROW
Year 2
Felt tip pen

4.39 WINDOW DESIGNS
Year 2
Assorted

4.40 WINDOW DESIGN PATTERNS
Year 2
Watercolour

5 Memory and imagination

5.1 FAMILY WEDDING
Year I
Tempera

INTRODUCTION

We have looked at some of the ways in which observation, investigation and research provide us with information. We can use the knowledge and understanding we have acquired to help us make things. We also need to recognise the importance of our existing experience. In any class there will already be a resource as rich as any we can provide – in the memories of the children. They will have come to school with their own individual experience of life and all this richness and variety should be valued, explored and used in their work in Art. We can tap into this resource and share our experiences by talking, asking questions and discussing events and ideas each time we begin a new piece of work.

This is called 'associative' knowledge and it is what each child brings to school not just when they begin, but as they grow and mature. Their lives at home and outside school can bring an added dimension to your whole class's understanding of any subject.

We need to have a variety of ways of sharing this knowledge and experience and your skill in being able to get each child to contribute will greatly enhance the sort of work they are able to do. In Reception classes, where the children have little or no written language, it is common practice to share all the events that happen outside school. We talk about home, birthdays, families (figures 5.1 and 5.2), pets and events and the class discussion time is greatly valued. It is informative, as well as giving the children an opportunity to gain the confidence to share their experiences, thoughts and feelings.

In Years 1 and 2 this activity continues but as writing improves it is more likely to be in the form of a written diary, progressively less of which is shared with others. So we tend to lose the sharing in an effort to concentrate on new knowledge and experiences coming from you, the teacher and from books and other sources.

Using the children's experiences in your lessons benefits more than just the work. It provides an opportunity for them to express their ideas

5.2 THE FAMILY
Year 5
Ceramic

5.3 **DRAGON**
Year 2
Collage

5.4 **DRAGON**
Year 6
Ceramic

and feelings, to know that you value them, their interests and their opinions. It should make them feel a part of what is happening in terms of the work you are doing because they have contributed to the shared knowledge and understanding on which that work is based.

The children's memories play an important part in the research you do for any topic, project or piece of work. Imagination is sometimes thought to be something people either have or haven't got. Again, understanding the nature of imagination will help us to see how we might best enable every child to know their thoughts are equally valid, that we don't regard some children as being innately more capable in terms of their ideas than others.

Imagination is actually a re-ordering of things we have seen in the past. If you try to think of something that has not existed before it has to be based on previous sights or experiences. For example, when we draw, model or write about mythical beasts like dragons, though they may be like nothing ever seen, they are always made up of parts of people and animals, reorganised and exaggerated (see figures 5.3 and 5.4).

Here, too, we need to be able to show children that their imagination and ideas are all equally valuable and that they have a real and important place in their drawing and painting. Memory and imagination are also the key to expressive work in art, craft and design. We need to understand how important it is for children to be able to put their feelings into pictures when it might be more difficult to express them in words. For example, we can show what it is like to be out in a storm and how it feels to be blown by the wind by using images before we have sufficient language to say and write as much (figures 5.5 and 5.6). But it is also true that we can communicate feelings in a different more immediate way by using visual images.

5.5 **THE STORM**
Year 2
Tempera

5.6 **AUTUMN**
Year 4
Water colour and charcoal

THE NATIONAL CURRICULUM

Memory and imagination are highlighted in both the End of Key Stage Statements and the Programmes of Study for the National Curriculum. They are written so that each statement in **Key Stage 2** builds on a related one in **Key Stage 1**. Thus progression is achieved and previous work built on constructively. For example, in the End of Key Stage Statements children in **Key Stage 1** are asked to record images from direct observation, memory and the imagination; in **Key Stage 2** they are asked to select and record images from direct observation, memory and the imagination using a range of materials and methods. Similarly in the Programmes of Study, Attainment Target 1, in **Key Stage 1** the children should respond to memory and the imagination; in **Key Stage 2** they should use a variety of recording methods to respond from memory and the imagination.

This evolving pattern of experiences needs to be one of the threads running through the work that you plan for the children. For example, in **Key Stage 1** a topic based on Spring might involve looking at plants growing and you could begin with something familiar. All expressive work is best if it is based on some actual observation or experience. The children could begin by looking at, talking about and drawing or painting some flowers, as in figures 5.7 and 5.8 where daffodils were used. In Reception and Year 1, not all the children will be able to count up to six so their daffodils may have lots of petals. It is worth remembering that when we looked at observational drawing one of the most important ways of getting to know plants was by counting the leaves, flower heads, petals and stems.

A group of five and six year olds were asked, following their observation work, to use what they had learnt about daffodils to make a picture

5.7 PAINTING DAFFODILS
Reception/Year 1

5.8 DAFFODILS PAINTED FROM OBSERVATION
Reception/Year 1
Tempera

5.9   DAFFODILS
Reception/Year 1
Tempera

5.10   DAFFODILS
Reception/Year 1
Tempera

showing their teacher where they most liked to see flowers in Spring. They talked about all the places where flowers might be seen – in markets, in their homes, growing wild and so on (figure 5.9). They had been encouraged to think of it in a personal way and one small boy chose to paint the flowers he had seen on his grandma's coffin in the churchyard some months earlier. He had never spoken of the event but his mother was very relieved that he was able to express his hidden feelings in a painting (figure 5.10).

In a more light-hearted but similar example, children in **Key Stage 2** made drawings of groups of apples showing how they look when seen together, with one apple overlapping the others (figure 5.11). Then, using

**5.11 APPLES DRAWN FROM
OBSERVATION**
Year 6
Oil pastel

5.12 APPLE
Year 6
Oil pastel
Drawn from observation and the
imagination

**5.13 APPLE DRAWINGS FROM
THE IMAGINATION**
Year 6
Oil pastel

**5.14 APPLE DRAWINGS FROM
THE IMAGINATION**
Year 6
Oil pastel

their imagination, they went on to show what they thought they might look like in a bowl on the sideboard or what might happen to those that were not picked but fell off the trees in autumn and were left to rot (figures 5.12 to 5.14).

When children return to drawing from memory rather than from direct observation they tend to return naturally to earlier drawing systems. They will be concentrating on the message they want to convey rather than on the drawing for its appearance. So it will help if you can support the subject matter of any expressive or imaginative work with some related resources and discussion which will help the children to think in visual terms.

MEMORY AND THE IMAGINATION

We have seen how, in a way, all drawings made from observation are in fact relying on short-term memory because we cannot look at the drawing and the object simultaneously. But when we are drawing from memory our whole attention can be on the paper and the lines and shapes we are making.

In **Key Stage I**, children will work freely from memory and enjoy using paint and colour without being concerned to try to make things look 'real'. They are able to express ideas directly using crayons or paint and to relish the marks as much for their own sake as for the message they are intended to convey (figure 5.15).

At this age, drawing and painting can be based on any experiences the children may have had like going to a swimming pool or a birthday party, or on things they have seen like birds or animals. For example, as in figures 5.16 to 5.18, imagine you are tiny and paint what you see. The children may find magnifying glasses useful here. Alternatively, an unusual feather has been found – it floated down from the sky and landed in the playground. After looking at it carefully and discussing the shape, colours and pattern make a drawing of the bird you imagine it came from.

5.15 MY FRIEND PLAYING
Reception
Tempera

5.18 PAINTINGS OF A PEACOCK'S FEATHER
Year 2
Tempera

5.16 PAINTINGS OF A PEACOCK'S FEATHER
Year 2
Tempera

5.17 PAINTINGS OF A PEACOCK'S FEATHER
Year 2
Tempera

5.19 DANCERS
Year 3
Tempera

5.20 TRANSFORMATION
Year 4
Felt pen

The children might also work on ideas from stories you have been reading; for example, fairy stories or those about imaginary events and places like haunted houses, enchanted forests or a secret garden. Poems offer a rich source of ideas and children's own stories can be illustrated, adding new information to the writing.

Some of these subjects are equally applicable in **Key Stage 2** , but children are likely to feel that the appearance of their work is important and want to make things look more recognisable and representational. So it is helpful to decide on the type of materials you are going to use and practise with them first. After talking and setting the scene it can be useful, too, to map out on a small scale how things are going to be arranged on the paper. We don't have something in front of us from which to work so we need to support this activity in other ways. Ask the children to imagine they are going to collect and order information from their memories, make small sketches of the things they want to put into their pictures, trying them out on a small scale. If any of the objects are available, the children can use them in their sketches to enhance their pictures. Having thought out the images, they can 'compose' them into a picture, adding detail and afterthoughts as they work (figure 5.19).

It gives children in this age group more confidence if they can plan and build their drawings or paintings gradually. They are more likely to succeed if they take it in stages rather than having to cope with all the problems of making a picture at once.

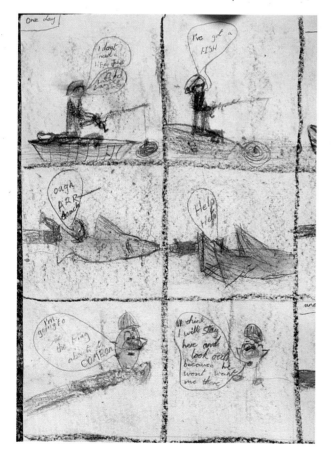

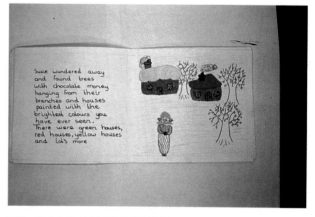

5.22 BOOK ILLUSTRATION
Year 6
Felt pen

5.21 DRAWING FOR INFORMATION
Year 5
Pencil and crayon
Part of a drawing telling a story
about sharks and a desert island.

Actually telling stories is another important way of drawing and children can use a series of sketches to show how things happen, like how to boil an egg, wire a plug or even what happens when a witch puts a magic spell on you (figure 5.20) or how they caught a fish (figure 5.21). Writing and illustrating their own stories (figure 5.22) is another avenue to be explored, giving opportunities for invention.

EXPRESSIVE WORK

This is different from imaginative work in that though it may be based on things seen by the children, like observation drawing, they will have shown not just what the object looked like but how they felt about it. All kinds of things make us feel happy or sad, threatened or joyful and children can find ways of expressing feelings through making drawings and paintings about them.

In **Key Stage I**, children are meeting so many things for the first time. They have to learn how people lived in the past and what they believed in. It is important that they have an opportunity not just to learn, but to express how they feel about all the things they are finding out.

History in the early years focuses on helping children to know about their locality. In a topic entitled 'A hundred years back' parents were asked to lend any items they had from that period. One grandmother contributed a fox stole from the 1930s and the children wrote about and drew it. They were horrified to think that ladies could actually wear a dead creature around their shoulders, simply for decoration (figure 5.23). Writing and making drawings about it gave them a chance to show how they felt (figures 5.24 and 5.25).

5.23 CHILDREN TRYING ON A FUR COAT

5.25 DRAWING OF A CHILD WEARING THE FOX FUR
Year I
Oil pastel

5.24 DRAWING OF A CHILD WEARING THE FOX FUR
Year I
Oil pastel

Key Stage 2 children feel just as strongly, but are more likely to be involved in wider issues. In this example the expressive work developed out of a topic the children were studying. They had been looking at the way the local industry of sheep rearing had affected the environment in which they lived. Having been out to the farm to see sheep being born and reared, they next visited the local livestock market and saw the sheep being sold (figures 5.26 and 5.27). They found the herding and selling of the sheep stressful and this is clearly reflected in the work they did following their visit (figures 5.28 and 5.29).

5.26 AT THE LIVESTOCK MARKET

5.27 AT THE LIVESTOCK MARKET

5.28 SHEEP IN A PEN
Year 6
Ceramic

5.29 SHEEP IN A PEN
Year 6
Ceramic

Other experiences can provide an equally strong influence in this age group and some children are more reticent about expressing their ideas and feelings in Key Stage 2 . Fiction-based work is a good way into expressive work for many children. In a topic based on *Carrie's War* they collected some black and white photographs of elderly people and the children made drawings from them, showing how they felt about age (figures 5.30 to 5.33). Equally, in *Racso and the Rats of Nimh* the children were able to demonstrate their dislike of these rodents (figures 5.34 and 5.35).

5.30 PHOTOGRAPH OF AN ELDERLY LADY

5.31 DRAWING FROM THE PHOTOGRAPH
Year 5
Chalk

5.32 PHOTOGRAPH OF AN ELDERLY COUPLE

5.33 DRAWING FROM THE PHOTOGRAPH
Year 5
Chalk

5.34 RATS
Year 5
Fibre tip pen

5.35 RAT
Year 6
Pencil

RESOURCING IMAGINATIVE AND EXPRESSIVE WORK

In order to stimulate the children's interest and fire their imaginations you will need to have available a wide selection of various types of resources.

We have already recognised how important it is to make use of the children's own knowledge and experience. It is also very helpful if they can be encouraged to make collections for themselves of things they find interesting that relate to the work you are doing. In looking for suitable subjects we should include:

● works of fiction, poetry and the children's own writing;
● historical and geographical material from our own area and any local features which can serve as a basis for storytelling;
● collections of objects on any visits you make which may spark ideas;
● folklore and stories connected with the past;
● festivals throughout the year.

Works of fiction

In the works of fiction, many of which you will have in your school library, you will find exciting descriptions of people, scenes, events and happenings and these can enrich the work children do both in their own writing and in the drawings and pictures that they make (figure 5.36). We can look for examples which open up wide ranges of possibilities, like *Alice in Wonderland* and Grimm's fairy tales to any by authors such as Roald Dahl. We can use many aspects of our drama lessons, based on stories we know or have made around a present crisis or event in the past, providing a powerful stimulus for the imagination.

Historical and geographical material

The history and geography of your area offers many clues to local happenings and to the way in which previous generations built the world we know today. Dressing up is one of the best ways to see what people from other times in history, or from other lands, really look like. If you have a collection of clothes or access to them through the school drama department or local theatre group, it will give the children a real starting point for work concerned with other times and places.

Probably your classroom already contains a collection of objects the children have brought in, but they can add to these by making use of visits in connection with other subjects. For example, on a visit to an area with woodland they might find fungi, twigs, bark and leaves; at a beach pebbles, seaweed, pieces of crabs, shells and limpets. Ambitious collectors might even find an old deckchair or bathing costume to weave stories around. In towns, they are more likely to come across the debris of everyday life but this can be just as rewarding. Imagine one of the children has found an old shoe. They could begin by wondering who wore it last, where it had been in its life and what might be going to happen to it next. Where was it made, who made it and what did they hope its future would be? Opportunities exist here for anything from sketches of the shoe in different times in its life to a full-sized painting of how the children imagine the owner of the shoe may have looked (figure 5.37).

Folklore, myths and legends

The stories, myths and legends which are particular to an area, country or civilisation can be a rich source of stories to fuel the imagination. Actual evidence to support these stories can be hard to find, as in the many versions of the tale of Robin Hood. However in churches and cathedrals in Britain we often find roof bosses and carvings of the green man, thought to be the spirit of the countryside or the forest. Stories about the origins of Morris dancing, the Maypole and many customs, both from this and other countries, are things which have fascinated and intrigued people for generations. Where these stories are part of any other subject you are studying, so that they have a focus for the children, they offer rich background for imaginative drawing and painting.

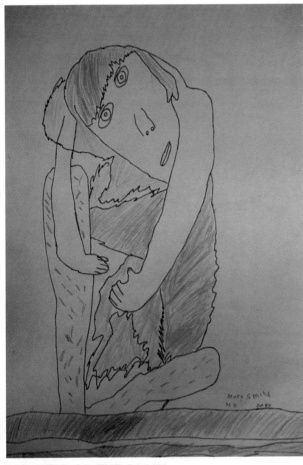

5.36 'STIG OF THE DUMP'
Year 2
Pencil and fibre tip

5.37 PIRATE
Year 5
Tempera

Festivals

Festivals which occur throughout the year in all religions offer a rich focus for expressive work. The stories are well known to followers of each faith so it is not only an opportunity to look afresh at these stories from the past but a challenge to try to make them come alive in a new way. For example, Christians celebrate Christmas and it is so familiar that stereotypes can creep in. One aspect you might look at is angels. Collect pictures of them as artists have portrayed them over the centuries. Since there is no definitive version, the subject offers an opportunity for children to draw and paint their own ideas, based on the works and ideas of others.

The Festival of Lights, called Divali in the Hindu religion, marks the return of Rama to his kingdom. The people light candles or small oil lamps along windows and balconies to welcome Rama home. It is a time when new clothes are worn, friends are visited and sweets exchanged. Paintings of lights, made soon after the experience and models or paintings which reflect the heritage of Hindu art all offer opportunities to extend the children's awareness of the richness of the past. Most religions have festivals which offer opportunities for making pictures, paintings and models about their seasonal festivals. They can be a real way of informing others and sharing our heritage.

In the case of the Muslim religion, Islam created its own styles of art and architecture. Because Mohammed preached against the worship of

5.38 PATTERNS
Year 5
Tempera

idols, Muslim artists were discouraged from making paintings or sculptures of people or animals. Instead they used designs based on flowers and plants, or geometric patterns like stars. They favoured fabric, jewellery and garden design and beautiful calligraphy. There is scope here to use the imagination in yet another way: to base learning about and making designs on the incredibly rich variety of atmospheres and feelings created by the skilful use of pattern and colour in Islamic art (figure 5.38).

THE IMPORTANCE OF TALK

The way you use words to create atmosphere, to set the scene and to focus the children's thoughts on the subject chosen will largely determine the results of their work. They cannot all be incredibly enthused by every subject but it is important with imaginative and expressive work that the discussion you have with them helps them to 'see' the scene they are going to draw, paint or make.

'Body' language is always important in teaching. If the children see that you have little interest in the activities you are asking them to do their response will be half-hearted and the resulting work of a low standard. Your contribution to all of their work is to be as enthusiastic about the subject as you would want them to be. If you believe in the importance of their progress they will succeed. Teaching with conviction involves being able to talk constructively about a subject, bring it to life for the children and show interest in their ideas. This is all especially important when you are asking children to work expressively and to use their imagination. If the work is to succeed then they must have confidence in your response to their efforts and know that you will take their responses seriously. The relationship between you and the children can and does affect their ability to work confidently.

In a practical way, too, you can help the children to work expressively by creating actual experiences for them within the classroom. One of the best descriptions of this occurs in *Rosegarden and Labyrinth* by Seonaid Robertson. She describes how a group of children were inspired to make very expressive and convincing clay figures of miners after covering some of their classroom tables with black fabric, creating a dark tunnel. The children had to crawl through the tunnel close together, not being able to see where they were going and experiencing the cramped conditions. She asked them not to talk about the experience immediately afterwards but to work directly into the clay. The work produced was full of feeling, with twisted and hunched bodies reflecting the children's reactions to the experience.

In a lesser way, but one which is still very effective, you can ask the children to close their eyes and try to visualise the subject or scene they are going to draw or paint (figures 5.39 and 5.40). With questioning, you can extend their ability to imagine by asking them to look at different parts of the scene, change it to another colour and to keep changing things around until they achieve a good solution. This is a skill which takes practice and will be rewarding when the children are able to do it with confidence.

Drama can raise awareness of what is happening in a way which is personal to the children because of the interaction between people in their concern for the event or the cause of the activity. Drawings and paintings made soon after the event can be full of the action and tensions and in discussion it is important to assure the children that in making a drawing or painting in this way the focus is on action and movement within the work, not on accuracy and tidiness.

To sum up, expressive and imaginative work relies on the quality of the stimulus, the discussion and the confidence with which the work is tackled. There should still be room for practising with materials and matching these to the subject being explored.

5.39 MINERS
Year 5
Tempera

5.40 MINERS
Year 5
Tempera

6 Collecting and organising resources

6.1 INDIA
Year 5
A collection of objects brought in by the class plus their models of Indian dancers.

6.2 COLLECTION OF OBJECTS
Year 3/4

SPACE AND ORGANISATION

Making collections of objects has figured in some way in most chapters in this book but you will appreciate the need to be well resourced in order to provide the stimulus needed for each piece of work. From modest beginnings and with the children's help, it should be possible to assemble sufficient basic items which will serve not just Art but many other areas of work.

Important considerations here are that you collect things which are genuinely of interest, relate to work in hand and organise them so that the children have access to them. Also, that you are able to make the most of them by displaying them effectively (figures 6.1 and 6.2).

Choosing what to keep and use depends, to some extent, on the particular circumstances within your school. Some classrooms have little room for displaying resources and even less for storage. So it will be necessary for you to adapt the principles outlined here to fit your situation.

There are various ideas and suggestions which may help in these circumstances. For keeping collections of objects, and some tools and art materials, you can use the relatively inexpensive, stacking plastic boxes which are for sale on some garage forecourts and in many stores and supermarkets. Some have lattice type sides and these are suitable where you want to see what is inside the box without lifting it down. Those with solid sides are more suitable for small, delicate or fragile objects. You could also choose to colour code them and keep different types of resources and materials in separate colours.

In small or awkwardly shaped rooms, it is particularly important to organise the wall and floor space. You should try to keep one area of wall or pinboard to display finished work, with the resources that the children worked from displayed beneath or nearby. That may mean that you have to have a small table by the pinboard on which to keep collections of artefacts (figure 6.3). This is clearly important because if the children are to appreciate that you want them to bring things in to work from then you have to make space for them to show how much you value their efforts. It may be that the rest of the room has to be rearranged but it will give you a focal spot where you can display and share each topic, project or sequence of work.

When you have established this 'exhibition' area and the children know and understand why it is important, then you will need to arrange the rest of the space to accommodate all the other necessary equipment. The various subject requirements are best kept together so that you have one area for all the Maths materials, one for Language, Science and the Humanities. This may sound like a council of perfection but is all the more important where space is limited. The crucial feature of organising your room is to see that children have access to all the tools, equipment and reference materials they need. At either extreme, where clutter prevents access or tidiness is put before the children's need to get at and use materials, learning will be hampered.

6.3 WASP, BEE AND BUTTERFLY DISPLAY

When you have established which areas to use for different subjects, try to find a space where you can pin up work in progress. In all the art work you do it is likely that you will have work that needs to dry or be stored until the next lesson. It is most useful if it can be on show so that the children can see it, from a distance, and have a chance to think about what they should be doing with it next. The opportunity to give this thought over a day or a week is preferable to instant decisions when the work is retrieved from a drawer. Visitors to your room will readily appreciate this and that classrooms should look like workshops, not exhibitions.

For three-dimensional displays, either of resources or clay models or constructions, you need to have available a series of small and medium boxes to change the height at which things are seen (see figures 6.4 and 6.5). Storage space is often a scarce resource so it is worth taking a little time to make your own display stands. Try to collect from supplies delivered to the school or from supermarkets a supply of sturdy cardboard boxes which nest together – four or five would be ideal. Cover them with any neutral coloured fabric, soft grey, greens, tones of blue or browns. Fabrics such as felt, hessian or old velvet curtains are suitable. Sew or stick the fabric down firmly on the inside, folding the corners to lie as flat as possible. When completed you can stack them, each one inside the other so that there is only the one box to store. Choose the size of the outside box to fit whatever space there is available in your room.

Another way of raising parts of a display of three-dimensional work would be to use bricks and planks of wood to form small shelves on a table or workbench. You also need to collect lengths of fabric and coloured papers, all designed to give a background which tones in with the overall colours of the items in the display (figure 6.7). Alternatively, you may have some bookshelves which can be used, where objects on display would be safe and need not occupy any floor space.

Some school buildings are fortunate enough to have purpose-built art

6.4   TRANSPORT DISPLAY

6.5   THEME DISPLAY: 'WHITE'

and design spaces and they certainly offer scope for practical sessions and space to display some of the work. However, this should not be a substitute for having the children's work in their own classroom where it can be reviewed, discussed and enjoyed as an integral part of their work, not as a separate, different activity.

MAKING COLLECTIONS

When you have organised the space and boxes in which to store the objects you need, with the children's help and involvement begin to collect things which will provide a stimulus. These should be not just for Art and Design, but things which will aid the children in understanding a range of ideas. These will fall into four broad categories:

● long-lasting objects, small and large scale
● short-term resources and living things
● borrowed things
● secondary source material.

The examples here illustrate different ways of using a few of the resources in some detail. They outline a variety of ways in which you might engage children's attention and interest in the objects.

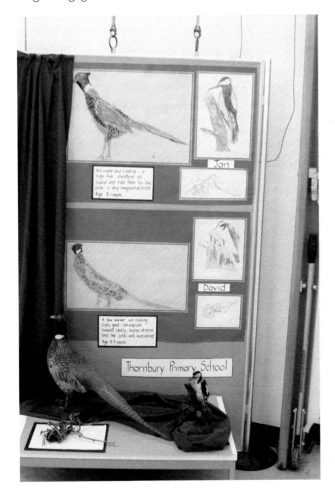

6.6 THE NATURAL WORLD – A DISPLAY

6.7 DRAWINGS OF BIRDS
Use of fabric, colour and focusing lines.

Long-lasting objects

In all the natural resources we use you can help the children to get to know and understand them by looking at a variety of aspects of the particular object (colour, form, shape, pattern, tone, texture, surface decoration, structure and growth). They can look for seasonal changes, erosion or damage and see how these have affected the object (figure 6.8). Of the long-lasting natural objects which we might expect to find in any classroom, small-scale objects will include shells, collected from the beach or in the case of a city school from the fishmonger, particulary those of whelks, mussels and cockles (figure 6.9).

The subject area you address depends on the sort of question you ask. For example, shells can be used for observational drawing and for imaginative work (draw the creature that might have occupied this shell after the original occupant left). For Maths they can be used for sorting into sets, colours and shapes. In Geography, you can ask where they come from, which part of the sea and which part of our coast or from other countries. In Science, you can be studying what sort of creature lived in each type of shell, looking at their life cycle and how they lived. Shells could also be used as a starting point for language work and storywriting. In all of this work, in each subject area, it is likely that you will want the children to make drawings or paintings looking at the shell from different points of view.

In a similar way, you might collect and use dried grasses and plants and flowers, leaves, seeds, bones (see figures 6.10 and 6.11), feathers, pebbles, bark, driftwood and pieces of wood with interesting grain and knots.

Made resources are affected by wear and tear and by how they have

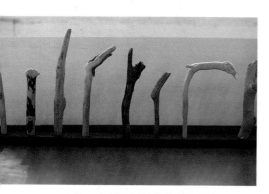

6.8   A COLLECTION OF WEATHERED TWIGS

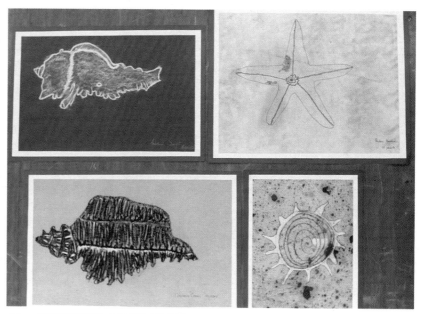

6.9   DRAWINGS MADE FROM DIFFERENT SHELLS
Year 5
Mixed media

been used. Some materials withstand ageing better than others. Long-lasting made objects can sometimes be those which have not been collected but are in everyday use in our homes and in school. We have looked at a variety of ways of using a shell; in our example this time we will look at various ways of using a teapot. This time, instead of different aspects of the object, we can learn about it from different points of view. We will also be learning a lot about the children and we will be able to tell from their drawings something about what stage they have reached in their perceptual development.

To set up the task you will need a teapot and a piece of paper folded in four and opened out again. Stand the teapot on the paper so that the spout and handle are directly over one of the folds. Give each of the children a piece of paper, any shape but folded into four, giving them space to make four quick drawings; they should number the sections from one (top left) to four (bottom right). Ask them to look at the teapot and draw what they see. Time the drawing, giving them about five minutes. After the first sketch, turn the teapot round a quarter turn in relation to the folded lines on the paper. The children should make three more drawings, in the numbered sections, with the teapot being turned each time. You will appreciate that as the spout and handle move round, the children see very different shapes.

6.10 COLLECTION OF SKULLS AND BONES

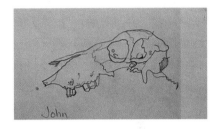

6.11 DRAWING OF A SKULL
Year 5
Pencil

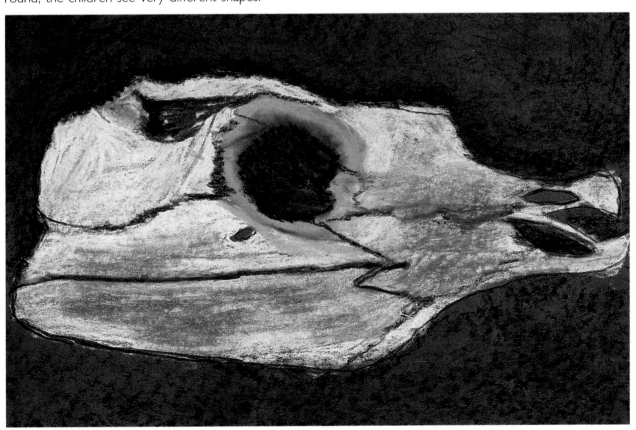

6.12 DRAWING OF A SKULL
Year 3
Chalk and charcoal

**6.13 PART OF A PAINT
PALETTE SEEN THROUGH
A MAGNIFYING GLASS**
Year 6
Tempera

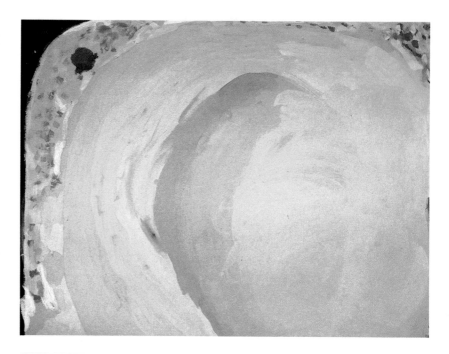

6.14 SPIDER
Year 4
Oil pastel

In *Knowledge and understanding in art* visual awareness and development are described in detail but here we need to understand that very young children will draw the teapot as they know it to be. Children's perception changes as they grow and the more perceptive child will see that, as it turns, they can see only part of the handle and spout – sometimes they disappear altogether. When you look at these drawings you will be able to see where the children are along this continuum – whether they have drawn the spout and handle in all of the sketches, because they know they are there, or whether they have drawn what they actually saw, that is with some parts of the teapot hidden.

Children move through these stages when they are ready and it should be interesting for you to know what level they have reached so that you are able to provide appropriate help and assistance. Using other resources in this way, looking at them from unusual angles, using magnify-

6.15 WOODLOUSE
Year 3
Oil pastel

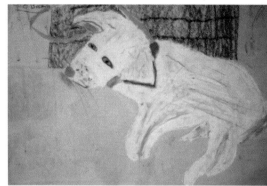

6.16 DOG
Year 5
Crayon

6.17 DOG
Year 6
Tempera

ing glasses and microscopes or just drawing a small part of something will help children to focus clearly on the object (figure 6.13).

Short-term resources and living things

Mini beasts are used in Science and can be an exciting focus for work in Art. For example, you might draw a spider in a jar or make models in clay from looking at snails (figures 6.14 and 6.15). Larger animals are also a good focus but you need to be sure they are fairly placid. Pet dogs and cats, hamsters and gerbils can all be drawn, painted and modelled (figures 6.16 and 6.17). For even larger animals you need to take the children on a visit so that they can make sketches to bring back to the classroom to work from. Safety is important here, both for children and the animals. Care needs to be taken to ensure that no problems arise.

Fish can be used in two ways: either in a fish tank, with wonderful opportunities to study refraction and distortion (see Matisse's 'Goldfish Bowl', no. 7 in the Resource Pack), or bought from the fishmonger, in which case they can be used for one or two days, if kept refrigerated (figures 6.18 and 6.19).

Fruit, vegetables and flowers are extremely versatile and can be used whole or cut into sections for observation or to use as a starting point for design. Imagine looking at slices of kiwi fruit, oranges, cucumber and tomato as a starting point for a design for a tray or tray cloth.

Fungi provide exciting possibilities for drawing, painting and modelling. The children will be fascinated by the immense variety of colours and shapes from tiny pearl-like white ones to the enormous bracket fungi which grow on trees and rotting logs.

Borrowed things

Museums, county collections, county resource services and local libraries

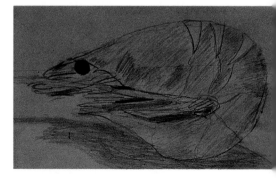

6.18 PRAWN
Year 3/4
Pencil

6.19 PRAWN
Year 3/4
Watercolour

6.20 OWL PAINTINGS WITH STUFFED OWL

offer us an opportunity to borrow from their collections. It is valuable to be able to have stuffed birds and animals, for example, for a term. The children can make drawings, paintings and models of them, learn about their life cycles and habitat and how, in this country, they are protected or treated (figures 6.20 to 6.22).

Photographs, slides and books are also important to give opportunities for research and the independent collection of information.

Secondary source material

Most important among secondary source materials are reproductions of works of art. It is essential that children have access to the work of others so that they may see how others have tackled a range of subjects. They learn about drawing and painting through looking at examples of other people's work in art and craft.

Reproductions of work in fine art posters, books and postcards are an essential part of any collection of resources.

Photographs are an important resource because, on one hand, they can be personal, taken by the children in support of visits they have made and helping to reinforce memories of the occasion; on the other hand, they could be, for example, of the children themselves and members of the family at different ages, building up personal pictures of the past and showing family likenesses.

Magazines and newspapers, encyclopedias, graphic books and comics will add to the range and variety of your collection, not only for the pictures they offer but also to cut up for collage material.

For expressive work you will need a collection of story books. Poems and music can provide a stimulus for the imagination.

Among the other printed materials you can collect are advertising posters (see figure 6.23) and other examples of graphic design including stamps, sweet wrappings and food packets, from the familiar cereal cartons to exotic creations like chocolate or perfume packaging.

6.21 FOX
Year 6
Watercolour
Painted from a museum specimen, with added background.

6.22 STUFFED BIRDS FROM THE MUSEUM, WITH SOME DRAWINGS

6.24 MAP OF AN IMAGINARY ROAD JUNCTION
Year 6
Tempera

Many sorts of maps are available and they can be used as examples of how to chart areas, describe the environment in a visual way and communicate information. Some of these will already be familiar, such as those in works of fiction like Narnia and Pooh's World; JRR Tolkien devised elaborate maps, and even a language for *The Hobbit* and the trilogy of books called *The Lord of the Rings*. In addition, you could compare Ordnance Survey maps with a variety of road maps to see how effectively they use symbols and signs. The children might be encouraged later to try designing their own, inventing signs and symbols to represent the things they want to put into their own maps (figure 6.24). Not all maps though need to contain symbols and signs. You could make environmental maps where the children collect information, rubbings, photographs and even samples of the things they pass on their way to school, to a park or on a favourite walk. They could use wholly visual information to record the journey. Alternatively, the children could make 'theme' maps showing, for example, where in their town (or nearest town if they live in a small village) particular facilities exist. They might make an aesthetic map showing where all the art galleries, museums, book and picture shops are or an entertainment map showing theatres, cinemas, swimming pools and sporting facilities are.

Playing cards offer a similar variety of opportunities for comparing, classifying, analysing and designing. The range of cards available include the standard 52-card pack, with numbers, suits and picture cards, to continental playing cards with 'blackberries' in place of clubs. Tarot cards are interesting examples of picture cards which tell stories; whereas there is a whole collection of picture, word and letter cards that go with particular children's games. You might ask the children to bring in any packs they have and use them as a basis for research, comparing the different games. The children could then go on to invent a game of their own and design and make the cards for it.

These are a few examples from a host of others.

6.23 PASTICHE OF A 1920S ADVERTISING POSTER
Year 6
Tempera

CHECKLIST OF RESOURCES

Using this list it should be possible for you to select sufficient items to have available in your classroom for the children to work from for the topics you plan for each year.

Visits provide an important stimulus; as do the experiences you organise for the children in your classroom and around the school. These together provide opportunities for the children to:

● draw, paint and model from direct experience;
● use a resource to generate ideas in a variety of materials and on different scales;
● make sketches and assemble information to make a composition in two or three dimensions;
● collect reference material in the form of sketches, notes, diagrams, maps and information on two or three themes and topics, to use as a basis for individual or group work in Art, on its own and for cross-curricular projects;
● add to their long-term visual memory and knowledge of the appearance and character of objects and the environment.

Long-lasting resources

Natural		*Made*	
small scale	large scale	small scale	large scale
Dried flowers	Houseplants	Balls of wool	Sewing machine
Dried grasses		& string	Old cash
Leaves		Toys	register
Eggshells		Teddy bears	Typewriters
Feathers	Pieces of wood	Dolls	Bird or animal
Bones	– with grain	Shoes, gloves,	cages
Bark		coats, hats	Parts of bicycles
Moss	Branches	Bricks	Wheels & tyres
Twigs		Glasses	Chimney pots
Pebbles		Bottles	Furniture
Stones		Kettles	Ropes
Sand		Shining metal	Lobsterpots
Tree seeds		objects	Car engines & parts
Oak apples		Mirrors	Tools – planes,
Acorns		Foilpapers	saws
Shells		Keys	Garden tools
Starfish		Padlocks	Musical instruments
Dried seaweed		Teapots	
Seeds		Cups	
Roots		Saucers	
		Hand tools	
		Screwdrivers	
		Kitchen tools	
		Can openers	
		Corkscrews	
		Nutcrackers	

Long-lasting resources cont.

Living/Short-term objects

School animals
Pond plants
    snails
    insects
    tadpoles
Mini beasts:
    Woodlice
    Grasshoppers
    Worms
    Insects
In cages:
    Gerbils
    Hamsters
    Mice

In school grounds:
    Hens
    Ducks
    School animals
Fish – in tanks or bowls
    from fishmonger
      – prawns, mussels, whitebait,
       sardine, sprats etc.
Fruit
Vegetables
Flowers, whole and cut up
Fungi
Wild plants (drawn in situ)

Borrowed resources

From your Museum Service or Resource Centre

Stuffed animals
Stuffed birds
Insects in cases
Photographs
Slide collections

Secondary resources

Reproductions of works of art
Book illustrations
Magazines
Photographs – from home & other
Graphic books
Books
Slides
Encyclopedias
Newspapers
(Music)
Maps
Playing cards
Posters
Stamps
Food cartons

School

The school building

Doors and door frames
Keyholes and letter boxes
Catches
Latches
Handles
Locks
Stairs, railings, balustrades

School pond or wildlife area
Plants, grasses, flowers
Creatures

School collection of dressing up clothes or costumes for drama/performances

Floors, stairs, corridors
Window and window frames
Lighting
Paving brickwood tiling – floor, wall and roof
Patterns, and textures and materials
Tubes, pipes and guttering

Resources which change in use
– to record every 5 minutes, 30 minutes, every day, once a week.

Candle burning down
Apples, fruit being eaten
Biscuits, cake being eaten
Twigs shooting and growing
Light fading (winter time)

Skies
Bulbs growing in a glass
Crystals growing
Mould growing on fruit or vegetables
Fruit and vegetables decaying

Quick sketches for information

Water running from a tap
Rain running down the window pane
Children running, dancing, playing
How people and things look outside when it is raining, blowing, snowing

Lighting

Torch or light shining on faces and objects from below, above and the side
Slide projector used to make silhouettes

The richness and variety provided by a well-resourced art education gives opportunities to work effectively within the subject itself and the subject as it informs and enhances so many others.

Visits to

Galleries	War memorials
Museums	Fountains
Heritage museums	Horse troughs
Theme parks	Shops
Mines	Beaches
Airports	Gardens
Farms	National Parks
Zoos	Nature walks
Wildlife parks	Hedgerows
Nature reserves	Lakes
Butterfly farms	City parks
National Trust properties	Town centres including
Castles	– pavements
Adventure playgrounds	street furniture
Theatres	names
Churches	lighting
Synagogues	postboxes
Mosques	litterbins
Cathedrals	signs
Town halls	

*Groups of resources for Art/
Technology*

Fastenings – latches, catches, bolts,
 padlocks, window handles
 – buttons, button holes, zips,
 velcro fastenings
 – toggles, laces

Support structures – scaffolding, pylons,
 bridges
Enclosures – fences, hedges, walls, trellis,
 barbed wire, wire netting, nets

USING RESOURCES TO GENERATE IDEAS

The immediate surroundings of your school, whether in a city, a village or, as in our example, a small town should provide enough reference material for you to be able to stimulate in the children a sense of enthusiastic enquiry. We have looked at ways of using focusing devices like viewfinders of different sizes and shapes, finding natural viewfinders like windows and doors to look through and ways of seeing familiar surroundings in a new light.

This example was called the 'Green' project and was centred on the hedgerow around the school though it could equally well have been looking at the playground, walls with plants growing on them and their colours and shapes. You could adapt this basic framework to the area around you, though it might turn out to be called 'Reds and yellows' or 'Browns and greys'.

At the beginning of this project the children were asked to talk about how they might encourage others in the school to be more aware of their environment and through that take more pride in keeping it tidy and well cared for. After some discussion they decided that they would show how attractive it was and make an exhibition to describe it to others. They began by looking carefully at the colours of the hedgerow and then to make those colours in a variety of different media. They used coloured pencils and oil pastels to start with (figure 6.25). They went out to the hedge and drew the colours in a small section of it (figures 6.26 and 6.27). With their drawings to help them and notes they had made, they were able to make some paintings of what they had seen using brushes, card and sponges, back in the classroom (figures 6.28 and 6.29).

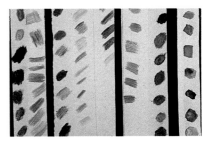

6.25 COLOUR MIXING CHART
Year 2
Coloured pencil, oil pastel and tempera

6.26 HEDGEROW COLOURS
Year 2
Oil pastel

6.27 HEDGEROW COLOURS
Year 2
Oil pastel

Next they found and cut up colour magazine pictures, carefully selecting all the greens they needed to make a collage (figure 6.30). Some children then went on to make an embroidery based on a leaf from one type of plant in the hedge (figure 6.31). The final exhibition had some work from every child and showed the many different ways in which the familiar surroundings could be explored and represented (figure 6.32).

In this project one idea led on to another. Through studying and representing the hedge in many different ways the children built up a better understanding not just of the hedge, but also of the materials they used to make their drawings, paintings and craft work.

DISPLAYING WORK AND RESOURCES

The principles and practice of display are only to be dealt with briefly here. This description of a few important points may help you feel that, far from being a daunting aspect of Art and Design, displaying work and resources is an integral part of the work. The really important function of displaying work is to show children how much you value what they make. Drawings and paintings are made for personal reasons but also to be seen and shared, not hidden away in drawers and folders. Learning about mounting and displaying drawings, paintings and craft work is also important to the children who should be developing these skills with your guidance.

6.28 HEDGEROWS
Year 2
Tempera

The order in which you might organise teaching the display of work is:

- trimming
- mounting
- putting up work
- using a variety of items.

Trimming

Often children start to make drawings and paintings on a standard sized piece of paper and then find they have only used a part of it. After discussion with you, by cutting off some of the edges, they can sometimes actually improve on the composition.

6.29 HEDGEROWS
Year 2
Tempera

6.30 HEDGEROW
Year 2
Torn paper collage

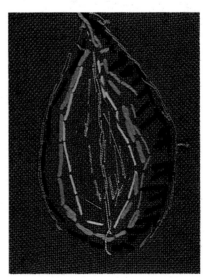

6.31 LEAF
Year 2
Fabric and thread

6.32 PART OF THE HEDGEROW DISPLAY
Year 2

Mounting work

Paper is an expensive resource. You can avoid wasting it by trimming 3 cm off two sides of the paper they are going to use. This will not materially affect the area the children have to work on but it does mean that when you come to mount their pictures you can use paper of the original size. When you take the display down, the work can be removed from the mount carefully, allowing this to be used for the next piece of work. In this way, no paper is ever wasted.

For trimming the paper use a rotary paper cutter which has lines printed on it, if you have access to one. This allows you to show the children how to cut their paper at right angles, positioning the paper in line with the block across the top and the lines down the cutter.

Using a felt tip pen to draw a 'focusing' line is the simplest but very effective way of mounting work, especially where space is at a premium (figure 6.33). Both single mounting and double mounting are effective. Glue will sometimes cause paper to crinkle so use double-sided cellulose tape or masking tape, folded back on itself to form a hinge. Use the opportunity to discuss with the children which colours will best show the work to advantage from the papers you have available (figure 6.34). For displays which explain the processes you followed, a variety of shapes and colours help the viewer to understand what the work was about (figure 6.35). Wherever possible, display the resources with the work so that immediate connections can be made by those looking at the exhibition (figures 6.36 to 6.38).

Putting up the work

For putting the work up you need just a few essential items. A plumb line, made from string and a small weight, will allow you to see if the work is vertical by holding it against the display board or wall. Staple guns or dressmakers' pins are preferable to drawing pins – they are less obtrusive and hold the work effectively. You need to have also some different types of staple extractor: the lever type marks work on the wall least; the claw type is useful for stapled sketchbooks and notebooks; and the plier sort will tackle most jobs. If you need to stick paper straight on to the wall, try using masking tape folded into hinges. It will not generally mark paintwork and leaves no greasy mark like some plastic adhesives.

Using a variety of items

Where possible use a variety of items in the display. Books, photographs and houseplants can bring added interest and make it more informative (figures 6.39 and 6.40).

The rewards and opportunities offered by having effective and informative displays in your classroom more than compensate for any time it may take for this to happen. It is important, too, that the children take part in choosing, mounting and arranging displays, with your help, guidance and encouragement.

6.33 FELT PEN LINES USED TO FOCUS ON COLOURED DRAWINGS

6.34 DOUBLE MOUNTING USING TONING COLOURS

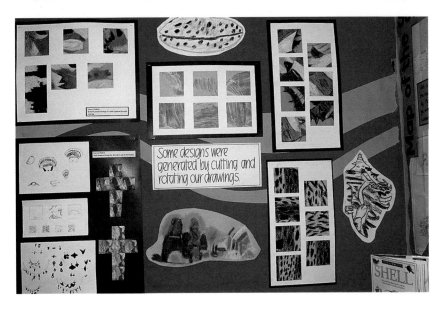

6.35 DISPLAY OF RESEARCH WORK

6.36 DISPLAY OF POPPY HEADS WITH THE PAINTINGS

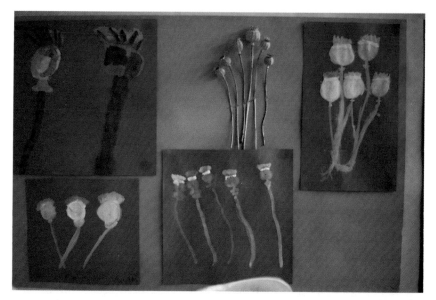

6.37 DISPLAYS OF DRAWINGS WITH THE RESOURCES

6.38 DISPLAYS OF DRAWINGS WITH THE RESOURCES

6.39 DISPLAY OF DRAWINGS WITH BOOKS USED IN THE RESEARCH INTO THE PLANTS IN THE SCHOOL PLAYGROUND

6.40 DISPLAY OF WORK, PHOTOGAPHS, RESOURCES AND PLANTS

Part 2

Making in art

Making art

1.1 CHILDREN MAKING PAINTINGS

SKILLS IN CONTEXT

Making is central to art. It is the manifestation of our thinking, feeling and response to the world around us. All worthwhile making is rooted in understanding and should be supported by investigation and research.

Art offers us a range of ways of learning, from observation and recording, to experimenting with and using different tools and materials to communicate our ideas (see figure 1.1). By understanding the work of others we can learn that our ideas have a common currency with people working now and in the past. This should be an important influence on our making; we can learn from others about different ways in which we might choose to express our own thinking and feeling. All making of quality, which reflects present thinking and leads on to other ideas, needs to be supported by research and investigation. For example, from the simplest recording of a flower if something new is not learnt, an opportunity is lost.

Making is concerned with how we shape our thoughts and put them down on paper or in other materials. If making is to be successful it needs to reflect our image of an object or idea we want to present to others. We need to learn how to do it effectively and to understand the range of skills associated with the subject.

In the following chapters of Part 2 you will be able to find out about an art vocabulary and what it means, what tools and materials you need to use and how to use them. The National Curriculum calls for no more, but indeed no less than this. It is every child's entitlement, as part of a broad and balanced education, that they should be able to understand art, craft and design. They should be confident and able to make use of the tools, equipment and techniques in this subject area. Confidence is

1.2 LILY IN A BLACK GLASS VASE

1.3 OBSERVED DRAWING OF THE LILY
Year 6
Oil pastel

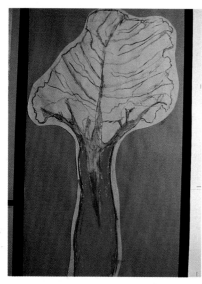

1.4   DRAWING OF A LEAF OF RHUBARB CHARD
Year 5
Pencil and watercolour

1.5   PAINTING OF A CRAB
Year 6
Tempera

vital. If children feel that they are likely to fail, because they have not been able to grasp what was required or how to cope with a task, then they will reject the subject on the grounds that it is a specialist interest. It is the right of every child to operate as effectively through Art as through any other subject. A child lacking confidence is barred from expressing a range of responses and you can see that this does not happen.

In the following chapters there are: explanations of the language you need to know, associated with the subject; the tools and equipment you will need to use with the children; and an outline of the way you can ensure that, when they leave you at the end of their primary schooling, they are on an equal footing with all other children going on to the secondary school. To identify clearly those aspects you need to know about, we will look at drawing and painting with a wide variety of different materials, print making, fabric work, graphics, use of Information Technology, clay work, construction, and many forms of three-dimensional work (see figures 1.4 to 1.7). The basics of each discipline are outlined in a way which will permit you to make a start. With an understanding of the requirements and techniques you will be able to read more about each individual area of expertise. Children in the primary school do not need experts in every field. What they most require is someone who can inspire an interest, carry them through the first steps with enthusiasm and engender a desire to know more.

Understanding art comes through making and children will absorb information through talk and practical activity. But to gain a depth of knowledge they also need to be able to evaluate their own abilities and progress. They need to be able to talk about their own work, the context in which it was made and also to compare it with their own previous achievements.

Confidence is important again here, from every point of view. There is a need to introduce an element of discussion in Reception and Year 1 so that children get used to talking with you and their peers about the drawings and paintings they have made. At a simple level, they can say what the picture is about and if they were able to put in all the things they were thinking about. First, it is important that they recognise that others share in their work and can talk about it. Second, it gives them the opportunity to practise and strengthen their confidence in talking to others in their group, in the way they already do in sharing news about home and personal events. The questions you ask should lead them to thinking about other things, what they might have included, or different ways they might have arranged the people and objects. This discussion is an important part of making. It will help them to appreciate that their ideas are for sharing, that they need to be open to comment and to other people's views.

Adapting and modifying work is always important. In the same way

1.7 CONSTRUCTION BASED ON A PAINTING BY HENRI ROUSSEAU
Year 4
Cardboard, card and paint

1.6 SUNFLOWER
Year 5
Ceramic

1.8 CHILDREN MAKING TEDDIES IN CLAY
Year 1

1.9 WORKING WITH 'EXPERTS' FROM NEIGHBOURING SECONDARY SCHOOL
Years 3 and 4

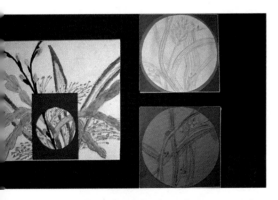

1.10 DRAWING, PAINTING AND CERAMIC FROM A 'HEDGEROW' THEME
Year 6
Mixed media

that children are encouraged to refine and redraft written work, so after discussion about their drawings, paintings and craft work they should become used to refining their initial designs. Learning skills is a gradual process and you will readily appreciate from your knowledge of this and other subjects that children need time to learn. It is important that you plan and structure their work so that they spend long enough on each activity to get a thorough grasp of the processes involved. For this reason, too, you will need to arrange for each new activity to build on previous knowledge. Skills learnt in isolation are easily forgotten and are certainly less effective than those built into a planned programme. For example, in clay work you could build on the children's knowledge of drawing, colour and form to introduce the skill of making a relief plaque for a decorative panel (see figure 1.10).

THE VISUAL LANGUAGE OF ART

Chapter 6 of *Principles and Practice in Art* discusses developing an art vocabulary and outlines the development of language in terms of the subject, showing how it can develop as children get older. Here we will look at what words and terms you need to know and clearly describe their meanings.

Line

This can be defined as making a continuous mark of any length and thickness which can be straight or curved, to describe a shape or form. For example, lines can be drawn with pencils, biros, felt pens, or brushes and in three-dimensional work in clay, plaster, lino or with fabrics (figure 1.11).

Tone

This is the depth of a colour or the density of the drawing in pencil, pen, biro, charcoal or fibre tip. The term can also refer to the overall appearance of a drawing or painting. For example, a painting in light tones will be gentle and bright whereas one in dark tones will be solidly painted (see figures 1.13 and 1.14).

Pattern

Regular patterns consist of sections of a design which repeat as in carpets or a row of rooftops (figures 1.15 and 1.16). Irregular patterns are those which are made up of a family of shapes. Examples of these sorts of patterns are: a pile of leaves together; the random patterns formed when logs are piled on top of each other; patterns on the shell of a tortoise or a collection of yarns (figures 1.17 and 1.18).

Texture

The surface qualities of an object or material – skin feels smooth, so do pebbles but the difference is qualified by the hardness of one and the softness of the other. Any woven fabric, collage or paper can be described in terms of how it feels to the touch – whether it is rough, smooth, prickly or sticky. Different types of paint also have distinguishable textures: for example, to take the extremes, oil paint put on with a palette knife can be rough and lumpy, whereas watercolour is hardly detectable on the surface of a strong paper.

1.12 TOWNSCAPE
Year 6
Pencil

1.11 LINE DRAWING OF A LOG
Year 6
Ink

1.13 PAINTING USING LIGHT
TONES
Year 4/5
Watercolour

1.15 SKYLIGHTS ON AN OLD
MILL ROOF

1.14 PAINTING IN DARK TONES
Year 1
Watercolour

**1.16 PATTERN TAKEN FROM
AN INDIAN CARPET**
Year 5
Watercolour

**1.18 COLOURED WOOLS FOR
SALE IN A MILL SHOP**

**1.17 PATTERN ON A
TORTOISE'S SHELL**
Year 1
Fibre tip pen

1.19   OWL COLLAGE
Year 2
Mixed media

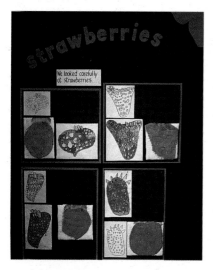

**1.20   FABRIC AND STITCH
WORK WITH SUPPORTING
DESIGNS**
Year 2
Mixed media

1.21   CORMORANT
Year 5
Oil pastel

1.22   VULTURE
Year 6
Watercolour

Shape and form

Shape usually refers to the outline of an object on the paper or in three dimensions. An object will have a different shape when seen from different points of view. We can compare and contrast familiar things and distinguish characteristic features by their shapes. Form is different from shape in that it refers to the whole volume or substance of an object as it is, not as it appears from different points of view (see figures 1.23 and 1.24).

Space

All forms of objects, natural and made, exist in space. For example, if you can imagine making a drawing not of the object but of the space around it or the shape of the space between two objects, then you would be describing space.

Colour

This subject is explored in chapter 6 of *Principles and Practice in Art* and also in some detail in Science in the National Curriculum. Children should be encouraged to use the correct names for colours so that they can describe them accurately. For example, they should be able to talk about the difference between cobalt blue (green blue) and ultramarine (purple blue), or crimson and vermilion (figure 1.25). Having a 'colour sense' can be thought of as knowing and understanding what colours you need in order to mix or make the ones you want to use. This comes through practise.

1.23 WALL
Year 6
Ceramics

1.24 WALL
Year 6
Ceramics

1.25 PAINTING OF A LANDSCAPE USING BLENDED COLOURS
Year 5/6
Watercolour

PROCESSES

As we have seen, drawing is central to all the work we do in art, craft and design. We need to be able to put ideas on to paper in order to plan and refine our designs to suit different processes. In planning you need to have in mind the process the children are going to use. It will help them to understand if you can have some examples for them to look at and discuss before they start their own work. In this chapter we will look at examples of drawing and design that led to work in batik, fabric, clay and print.

Textiles

The different processes here range from fabric printing and batik, which involve working on and changing ready-made cloth, to weaving in which fabric is actually created. In the first example, children have been encouraged to look at and make drawings of themselves and use these as a starting point for batik. This is similar to painting but uses hot wax and dyes instead of paint. The children looked at examples by well-known craftworkers before beginning (figure 1.26). In the second example, the children looked at a stuffed owl and made drawings, in oil pastels, looking particularly at the patterns created by the feathers (figure 1.27). Then using watercolour and pencil they looked specifically at individual feathers to find out what patterns and colours they contained (figure 1.28). The whole investigation culminated in a piece of weaving showing patterns the children had found in the owl (figure 1.29).

Steven and Natasha drew pictures and dyed themselves in daytime colours.

1.26   DRAWING AND BATIK
Year 1
Fibre tip pen and batik

1.28   PAINTING OF FEATHERS
Year 4
Watercolour

1.27 OWL DRAWING CONCENTRATING ON PATTERN AND TEXTURE
Year 4
Oil pastel

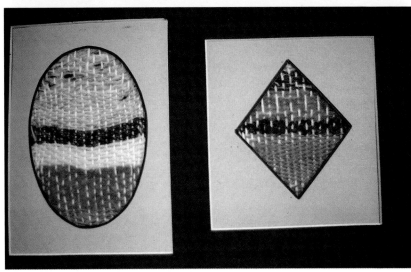

1.29 WEAVING BASED ON THE COLOUR AND PATTERNS OF THE OWL
Year 4
Coloured yarns

Clay

Figure 1.30 shows that the children began by looking closely at the patterns on the dragonfly. These were translated into clay – in the first instance, on flat tiles which gave the children the chance to concentrate on the pattern and shape (figure 1.31). This was then extended to work in three dimensions, involving the skills of joining and modelling. The children found this task easier to handle due to the previous experience in relief (figure 1.32).

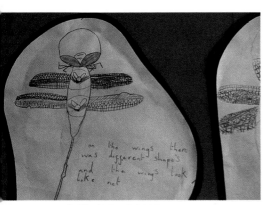

1.30   DRAGONFLY
Year 1
Biro

**1.31   RELIEF MODELLING OF A
DRAGONFLY**
Year 1
Ceramic

1.32   MODELS OF DRAGONFLIES
Year 1
Ceramic

Textiles and clay

In this example of a sequence of work, the children began by visiting a local bridge. It was, in fact, the original 'Ivy bridge' that gave their town its name. They made pencil drawings of some parts of it and a coloured drawing using oil pastels (figure 1.33). In school, they were able to make watercolour paintings from the information in their sketches. They could then carry out designs in felt and decorative stitching as fabric pictures or make ceramic number tiles for their houses (figures 1.34 to 1.36).

1.33 DRAWINGS OF A BRIDGE
Year 5
Pencil and oil pastel

1.35 FABRIC DESIGNS BASED ON DRAWINGS OF THE BRIDGE
Year 5
Felt and coloured threads

1.34 THE BRIDGE
Year 5
Watercolour

1.36 PLAQUE BASED ON DRAWINGS OF THE BRIDGE
Year 5
Ceramic

Print

Drawing is also important here. In this example the children went out to look at houses in the locality. They chose one house each and made a study of the various patterns and textures of brick, stone and tiles (figure 1.37). This was followed by a drawing of the front of the house (figure 1.38). In school they used their drawings as a basis for print making (figure 1.39). They had to remember that when a print is made the drawing comes out the opposite way round – vitally important especially if there are any letters or signs in the design.

REFLECTION AND REVIEW

It is important always to be sure that the children have understood the purpose of the work they have been doing and know why it was important they had that particular experience at that time. It will build confidence if they know that each piece of work fits into an overall plan designed to give them a thorough knowledge and understanding of Art and an opportunity to learn all the skills and processes.

Instead of finishing a lesson or piece of work with clearing up, do that first, then you can end the session with ten minutes of discussion of successful outcomes. It can be seen as a time when you reinforce the importance of what the children have learnt and experienced. The children can have an opportunity to recap on any points they were not too sure about or may have missed. Children are becoming increasingly familiar with self-evaluation and it can be used very productively in these circumstances. You need to encourage them to comment constructively on each other's work in the same way that they should be coming increasingly familiar with looking at and commenting on works of art and craft.

This is another excellent opportunity for language development. You can begin to introduce words which will accurately describe colour, use of techniques and descriptions of the tools and materials that artists use. It should form part of the research that the children do as they tackle each new area of work. For example, in print making (as described in chapter 4), they could learn about the different ways in which prints are made, what tools and equipment each process requires and how the printing methods are different from each other. Making is always better and likely to be more successful if it is founded on a thorough knowledge of the process and an appreciation of suitability of the method to the ideas being expressed. In other words, it equips the children to make sound, informed choices of the ways in which they want to express their ideas.

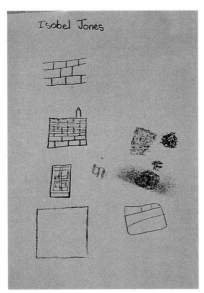

1.37 DETAIL OF A HOUSE
Year 6
Pencil

1.38 DRAWING OF A HOUSE
Year 6
Pencil

**1.39 PRINT MADE FROM THE
HOUSE DRAWING**
Year 6
Ink

Drawing

2.1 CHRISTENING DRESS
Year 2
Fibre tip pen on white paper
To show the use of contrasting
tools and materials.

AN INTRODUCTION TO DRAWING

Drawing is the central core of all work in Art. Drawings were made by people in different civilisations to communicate information and ideas, long before there was any written language.

There are many ways in which we can all describe things and communicate ideas through drawing if we have sufficient skill. Acquiring these skills is comparable with acquiring language and there are many similarities in the process. Drawing depends on an individual's confidence in their ability to 'say' in a drawing what they want to convey to others. This skill is developed through frequent practice and the correct guidance. All children who can hold a pencil can make marks with it. The quality and meaning invested in those marks is something that depends on constructive teaching and progress in understanding how to use the tools and techniques (see figures 2.1 and 2.2). From Reception on, all children will be able to make progress in drawing if the tasks you set them are appropriate. The following chapter sets out to show how those tasks may be structured in order to give every child the opportunity to develop his or her own ability.

Not all children will be equally successful. As in other subjects, like language for example, there are those who excel and those who find it less easy. But all of them can reach a basic understanding and learn what the subject has to offer in communicative and expressive dimensions.

2.2 CHRISTENING DRESS
Year 2
Chalk on black paper

MARK MAKING

In every aspect of drawing there is a variety of tools and grounds that you can use. The 'tools' include pencils of various sorts, pens, brushes and any other implement that will make a mark. Van Gogh did some of his drawing with ink and a sharpened reed. You can see one of his drawings in the Resource Pack: 'Landscape near Montmajour' (no. 13). Quills have been used by monks for centuries. Goose and swan quills are popular because they are easier to handle than smaller ones. We will look at ways of using various tools and match them to suitable grounds.

'Ground' refers to the sort of paper or material on which the drawing was made. In the Middle Ages, when drawings were made in manuscripts, monks used parchment or vellum which were made from carefully prepared animal skins. Now we have a wide variety of manufactured papers on which to work. It is important to choose paper which will support the work you are asking the children to do. If, for example, they are going to use ink you would need to use cartridge paper because a less substantial surface might crinkle with the application of ink or it might be torn by a sharp pen-nib. In either case, the drawing would be less than satisfactory and the work you plan for children needs to lead to success, not failure.

Whatever you choose for the children to work on, they will need to get used to thinking about and discriminating between the qualities of the tools they are working with and the 'grounds' they are working on.

2.3 'STIG OF THE DUMP'
Year 2
Pen, brush and ink

Pencils

Pencils come in different types of lead: H stands for hard lead and B for the degree of blackness that the pencil will make. The range is large and goes from 9H, which is extremely hard and makes a fine greyish mark (used by draughtsmen and architects who need absolute accuracy), to 9B which is very soft and gives a soft, black mark which will smudge and form dark tones. For all practical purposes you need to have available for the children to use an HB, 2B and 4B or 6B. In addition, you may like to use the fatter, soft-leaded pencil – like 'Black Beauty' or Alphex – with younger children or when you want a soft sketching pencil.

Introduce these ideas by explaining to the children that though they are familiar with pencils as writing tools, in fact pencils are actually capable of making a very large range of marks. For example, you might try out some of these tasks:

● Ask the children to see how many different lines they can make, using each of the three grades of pencil; then how many tones or spots. Use a good quality white paper for this, even though it is practise. The children need to be able to see the variations in marks very clearly.

● Then ask them to see how many different marks they can make, using the pencil on its side or its end. Pressure can affect the sort of mark that all graphic tools make and the children need to be able, consciously, to control the amount of pressure they exert on their pencils or other media. Ask them to make a line which curves up and down, pressing hard on the down strokes and very lightly on the up strokes. This should produce an effect which makes the line appear to undulate, like a wave.

2.4   HEDGEHOG
Year 5
Pencil

● Ask the children to try making tones with different grades of pencil. In the same way that they were able to make lines of different appearances, they can now make a variety of tones from light to dark and from thick to thin. Follow this by looking at things which have lines covering their shape, like hair on an animal (figure 2.4) or looking at each other's hair and clothes (figure 2.5). Ask the children to use their pencils to make long or short strokes which follow the form of the person or animal. By following the shape and getting the lines to curve they will be able to make their drawing look as if it has some depth and form. If you choose a subject which is light against a dark background – like pale fruit or flowers on a dark tablecloth or a figure dressed in light clothing – the children can explore ways of using pencil to create the darkness behind the object, showing how it can make the whole effect of the drawing more dramatic and interesting (see figures 2.6 and 2.7).

2.5   PORTRAIT OF MY FRIEND
Year 4
Pencil

● Another technique the children can try is cross hatching, that is drawing one set of lines close together in one direction, followed by another set of lines over the top in another direction. Many book illustrators use this technique. Look at examples of work by Michael Foreman and Jill Bennett, or those by Edward Ardizzone in Clive

2.6 JUDO FIGURES
Year 4
Pencil

2.7 JUDO FIGURES
Year 4
Pencil

2.8 CHALK AND CHARCOAL DRAWINGS
Year 2

King's *Stig of the Dump*. Make it clear that this sort of practise is essential if they are to get to know the variety of marks they can use to make their drawings.

● An invaluable resource in mark making is to look at drawings by artists who have explored this. Van Gogh has already been mentioned but it is worth taking the time to find reproductions of the drawings he made of the countryside. Henry Moore drew sheep in the landscape and Paul Klee drew in continuous lines to describe town scenes and the countryside, while David Hockney uses a remarkable range of marks in his drawings of gardens and swimming pools. Make a collection of drawings by artists that the children can use for reference and information.

Charcoal and chalk

In a similar way, when you introduce charcoal and chalk it is important to practise (see figure 2.8). Ask the children to begin by making lines and tones in chalk. You will find that when they begin to experiment with charcoal the marks are often so dark that they lose their definition. By beginning with chalk you will be able to encourage them to blend the charcoal in so that it creates light and shade (figure 2.9). For example, you need to suggest ways in which they can experiment. In all of the instructions below they should practise with the chalk first, then with charcoal, and use grey or buff paper so that both chalk and charcoal stand out from the background.

One of the characteristics of chalk and charcoal is that they will smudge. There are two important aspects to this. First, we need to see that drawings are not spoilt by being leant on as work progresses. For this you need to provide the children with small pieces of paper that

2.9 PRACTICE SHEETS
Year 5
Pencil, chalk and charcoal

go between their hands and the drawing so that their hand rests on the paper, not the drawing. Second, you should give the children an opportunity to draw lines of chalk and charcoal next to each other and smudge one into the other as a controlled activity. You may be able to find examples of work by well-known artists who have used this technique. Many artists have used these materials, including artists from different periods in history like Rembrandt and Bonnard. Try to look at the work of Toulouse-Lautrec, Degas, Matisse, Auerbach and Kossof (one of whose paintings is in the Resource Pack – no. 2).

2.12 DRAWINGS FROM A STUFFED FOX
Year 5
Chalk and charcoal

● Ask the children to make a line so light that it can hardly be seen. Then add lines which get stronger and stronger each time. Do not press so hard that you break the chalk. It is preferable to make several marks in the same place to make it strong and clear. Then practise making tones, again starting with light ones and gradually making them stronger.

● To begin to make shapes, practise with a sphere and matchbox. Draw the sphere in chalk first, then add lines which follow the contour of the shape. Lines which go from side to side will make the object appear flat. Add the charcoal to give it depth and make it appear solid. To put this into practice choose objects which have some black and white, or black with light on them and ask the children to make drawings of them. They should always start with chalk and add charcoal to give it form and shape (figures 2.10 to 2.12).

● Other black and white drawing tools you might introduce when the children are thoroughly competent in using chalk and charcoal are conte crayons and graphite sticks. Both make individual and characteristic marks which contrast with the more familiar sorts.

All soft tools like chalk and charcoal need 'fixing'. As these materials are so soft they will smudge and this is part of the joy of using them.

2.10 UMBRELLA
Year 5
Chalk and charcoal

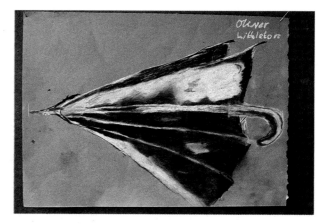

2.11 UMBRELLA
Year 5
Chalk and charcoal

However, when the drawing is finished it needs to be made 'permanent', so that it will not be spoilt by handling. There are effective fixatives which can be sprayed on to the work – and they are environmentally friendly! If these prove to be too expensive, you will find that a not too highly perfumed hairspray makes an acceptable alternative.

Biros, fibre tip pens and pen and ink

Once again, these are predominantly black and white media. The advantages of working in some kind of ink means that the marks are permanent and therefore call for special concentration because there can be no temptation to rub them out.

Subjects which work particularly well in inks are any which call for fine and clear detail. Just as with other tools, the children should practise to see how many different marks they can make. They will find, if they are fairly adventurous, that the range is surprisingly large (see figures 2.13 to 2.15). Indeed children can achieve free and lively drawings that have a quality of spontaneity about them. The drawings will also photocopy well, unlike pencil sketches. If they are used as a starting point for design work the children can keep their original drawings and try out variations on the photocopies (figures 2.16 and 2.17).

Crayons and pastels

There is a wide range of dry colour media – all useful because the whole class can work together, mixing and blending colours to match resources, without the organisation needed to work with paint.

● Wax crayons are used to draw with in the early years because they are easy to handle. You can encourage the children to blend them to make the colours they want and to explore ways of making different textures with them. For example, they can be used to make coloured line drawings or used thickly to fill areas with colour.

2.13 MY HAND
Year 6
Biro

2.15 MUSICAL INSTRUMENTS
Year 6
Biro

2.14 MUSICAL INSTRUMENTS
Year 6
Biro

2.17   DESIGN FOR ADVERTISING POSTER
Year 6
Pen, brush and ink

2.16   DESIGNS FOR ADVERTISING POSTERS
Year 6
Pen, brush and ink

2.18   CYCLAMEN
Year 2
Oil pastel

● Oil pastels and coloured pencils can extend this range of mark making into more subtly blended colours. Beginning with practising with the tools, you could ask the children to try out and compare the sort of marks they make and what sort of grounds you might choose to use them on.

The following examples show the contrast between the two types of tools and illustrate some of the ways in which you might use them. In figures 2.19 and 2.20 the children were asked to find out how the media work and how they are different from each other. The choice of ground is important: pencil crayons – even those of the best quality – take time to make strong colours and are therefore best used on good quality white paper; pastels can show to best advantage on a dark or coloured ground. Let the children try them out on different grounds so that they understand and can make their own choices of the best background to work on. In the case of oil pastel, they will find that they can create two ranges of colours by using the pastels on their own, or with white pastel drawing underneath the colour, which makes it brighter and clearer.

Having experimented with tools and grounds, in the second of our examples we will look at working from two types of resources. This should give a clear understanding of the different characteristics of the two types of tools. In the drawings of birds in figures 2.21 and 2.22 pencil crayons were used to draw a faint outline. This enables the children to position the object, and get the size right in relation to the paper. If it is drawn in a light colour first, the drawing can be altered if necessary, without causing a problem. In pastel, the same things apply. If the drawing is made first in white or yellow, the children can change their minds and redraw sections to fit the paper better without having to start again.

2.19 PRACTICE SHEET
Year 2
Pencil, crayon and oil pastels

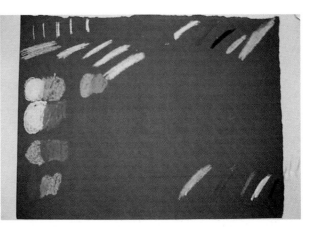

2.20 PRACTICE SHEET
Year 2
Oil pastels

**2.21 DRAWING OF A STUFFED
DUCK**
Year 2
Coloured pencil

2.22 DRAWING OF A DEAD JAY
Year 4
Oil pastel

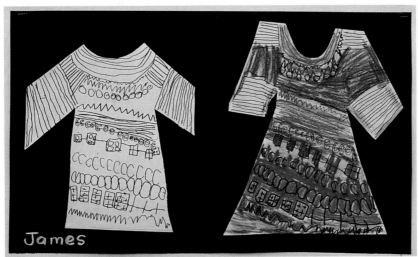

**2.23 COSTUME DESIGN FOR A
PARTY DRESS**
Year 1
Fibre tip pen and coloured pencils

2.24 TEACHER'S COAT
Year 5
Oil pastel

2.25 'LINES' EXHIBITION

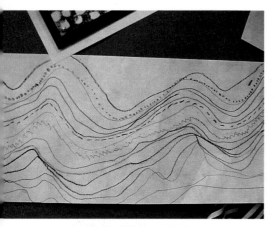

2.26 LINE DRAWINGS
Reception and Year I
Mixed media

2.27 LINE DRAWINGS
Reception and Year I
Mixed media

In the last example, looking at a made resource, we can see the contrast between pencil crayon and oil pastel. We can look at the way children have been able to use these tools to draw the objects that interested them. The costume design (figure 2.23) focuses on line and colour; the drawing of the teacher's much loved and valued coat is a super example of tone (figure 2.24).

Other dry colour media you can use in a similar way, experimenting on different backgrounds, are plastic crayons and chalk pastels. Plastic crayons work much like coloured pencils and chalk pastels work well on a rough surface but need fixing (as did the chalk and charcoal drawings).

MATCHING MATERIALS AND GROUNDS TO IDEAS

In the last chapter we introduced some ways in which you might encourage the children to think about choosing different tools and materials for different purposes. In a little more detail we can look at two projects where they were encouraged to think about materials on an equal footing with the subject matter.

In one study in black and white the children began by making a collection of all the things they could find with lines, in every type of material. These included lines on fabrics, lines drawn and printed on paper and in books and those they could find in their classroom and around the school (figure 2.25). They wrote lists of words to describe the particular qualities of the different lines and then went on to choose the sort of mark-making tool that they thought best suited each type of line. They looked for things like the width or thickness, solidity and grain of each sort of line. Then they tried out the pencils and pens they had chosen on different sorts and textures of paper, ending up by choosing a good quality cartridge with a slightly textured surface. They went on to make drawings of all the different kinds of lines they had been able to discover (figures 2.26 and 2.27).

Then the children made prints, using black ink on white paper from blocks made by drawing into 'press' print blocks (figures 2.28 and 2.29). Again the types of ink and paper were part of the discussion, as were the qualities of the prints that were made.

In the second example, the children began by looking at some reproductions of flower paintings by Bernard Buffet. They were interested in the transparent qualities of the paint he had used and in how the effects were produced. To match some of the characteristics of the painting they chose to use a wax-resist method. The children tried out various tools but chose coloured pencils as these best matched the quality of the coloured inks they would use in making their pictures.

Next they made some drawings from the painting to find out how it had been composed, trying to match the arrangement of the vase and flowers on the paper (figure 2.30). Then they made drawings from real flowers as a starting point for designing their own pictures. They chose smooth white cartridge paper because this would best show the qualities of the resist. Having done all the research into subject matter and materials the next step in the process is to make the drawing in wax crayons or oil pastels. When the drawing is completed, coloured inks are mixed with water and brushed over the top of the drawing (figures 2.31 and 2.32).

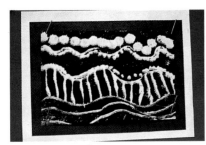

2.28 BLOCK PRINTS
Reception and Year 1
Water-based printing inks

2.29 BLOCK PRINTS
Reception and Year 1
Water-based printing inks

2.30 DRAWING FROM A REPRODUCTION OF A PAINTING
Year 4
Coloured pencils

2.31 FLOWERS
Year 4
Oil pastel and coloured inks

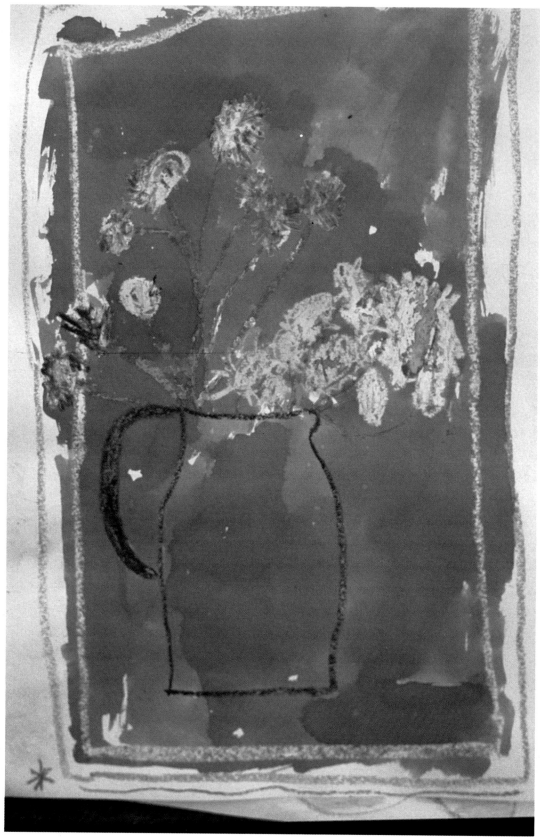

2.32 FLOWERS
Year 4
Oil pastel and coloured inks

DRAWING FOR DIFFERENT PURPOSES

Drawings are made for a multitude of purposes and satisfy needs that cannot be fulfilled in any other way. They can:

- describe and record how things look
- communicate ideas, give instructions visually and convey information
- analyse the natural and made world to see how it works or is made
- tell stories about experiences
- express personal ideas and feelings.

Different subjects demand drawing for their own purposes and the skills required need to be taught in art lessons. For example, in language, fiction and poetry the children will need to work through all five functions – writing and drawing about things seen, felt and experienced. In Science they need to observe, analyse and communicate and in Humanities they need to be able to look at real artefacts, to record them accurately, explain how they came to be and where they fit into the world, past or present.

In Part 1, these different functions are described in some detail and examples are given of how you might use them. It is important to plan your programme of work in order to make sure that the children are involved with all these aspects of drawing as each fulfils a different purpose and involves different styles and techniques. Checklists offer one way of ensuring that the balance between the observing and analysing, informing and expressing is maintained.

As a last example, we can look at a cross-curricular project which was concerned with the building of an outdoor classroom at a city school. It involved Language, Maths, Science, Humanities and Art. This part of the project was concerned with planning the area, building a pergola, planting and growing the plants to climb up it (see figures 2.33 to 2.36).

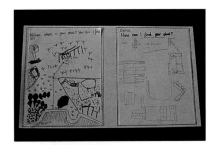

2.33 HOW CAN WE FIND THE PLANTS?
Year 2
Mixed media

2.34 THE SCENE BEFORE THE PROJECT BEGAN
Year 2
Tempera

2.35 THE PERGOLA HAS BEEN BUILT
Year 2
Tempera

2.36 WHAT WILL IT LOOK LIKE WHEN ALL THE PLANTS HAVE GROWN?
Year 2
Tempera

Painting

3.1 POWDER COLOUR, PAINT TRAY AND BRUSHES

AN INTRODUCTION TO EQUIPMENT AND MATERIALS

Choice of paints, brushes and palettes can aid the teaching of painting, as can management, care and storage of all the equipment involved. Success is founded not only on good teaching but on having the right tools and materials available.

Paint

Powder colour is by far the best choice for colour mixing. Dry colour makes mixing paint necessary because it cannot be used straight out of the pot. Water has to be added and this means that children are involved immediately with the process. Success also depends on having the right containers. Purpose-made pots are the cleanest to use. These are available from some of the major suppliers (figure 3.1). The individual pots are removable for cleaning and filling. (Bun tins or shallow pots are not suitable as paint will be carried from colour to colour on the brush.) Paints can be shared so one set between two children means 15 sets would be enough for a class of 30 should you want them all to paint at the same time.

These pots come in sets of six so it would be convenient to have six colours. This matches what you need for colour mixing in the primary school. You should have white, brilliant yellow, two reds (vermilion and crimson) and two blues (cobalt or cyan and ultramarine). This combination makes it possible for the children to make all the other colours. When you order the paint, buy twice as much white and yellow as these are used most quickly. Black is not included because black powder paint, for reasons of manufacture, is difficult to mix with water – so black squeezy or readymix paint is recommended. This has an advantage as you can control how much the children have by keeping it yourself and dispensing it on to their palettes when they need it. Because nothing in nature is as black as black paint, it is good to have control of how much is available. The black made from the colours in the paints the children have will blend in far better in paintings. Colour mixing will be described in more detail in the next section.

Using powder colour needs to be taught. Brushes are dipped into water, touched on the edge of the pot to remove any surplus and then dipped into the powder paint. This is transferred to a mixing palette and the process repeated. Too much water on the brush makes the paint wet and this needs to be avoided.

Brushes need to be washed between making each colour and everything should be kept clean. Generally, it will be best to begin with the lightest colour first and add the darker one to it. At the beginning of a lesson small pieces of the same paper as that to be used for the painting should be available for the children to experiment on. They need to see how thick or runny to make their paint and what it looks like on that particular paper.

Paint blocks are easy to use but wasteful to keep clean and more

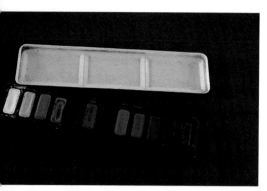

3.2   WATERCOLOUR BOX

difficult to use for colour mixing – they are very hard on brushes too! The colours tend to get stronger as the water penetrates the block and this makes it difficult to control the amount you need to make other colours.

Squeezy or readymix paints in bottles mix quite well but as they are liquid there is a tendency for children to use them straight from the bottle rather than to mix them. If you already have large stocks of these to use, you need the same range of colours as specified for powder colour (see above). The larger the range of colours you have available the more likely it is the children will use them straight from the container. Then they will be satisfied that, for instance, a green is nearly right; whereas with dry powder they can learn to make exactly the right green.

Watercolours are best bought in boxes (figure 3.2). They have a good range of colours and can be used straight from the box. When you buy them also order some replacement watercolour tablets – as with other paints always order twice as much white and yellow.

Palettes

Children need to have one palette each for mixing paint. Flat plastic dinner plates like those for school meals are the most easily used. All purpose-made palettes with divisions and ridges are much more difficult to wash out and are best used where large quantities of paint are required at one time. For most purposes, a flat plate provides more area for mixing and is easily washed and re-used.

A simple plate drying rack can be used. Palettes can be stored and are dry and clean for use each time. Boxes of watercolours have lids which are designed to be used as palettes and these are easily cleaned too.

Brushes

As with all equipment the better the quality the more easy and satisfying the brushes are to use. Some of the cheapest now available are too soft and therefore difficult to control and quickly lose their hair. Nylon filament brushes hold their shape well and are most economical in the long term. A variety of shapes and sizes is essential. Children should be provided with three different brushes for each painting task. The sizes will vary with the scale of the painting they are making. You will find these illustrated in catalogues from all the major suppliers. You need a range of sizes in short-handled brushes for watercolour and for fine details on larger paintings, flat and round long-handled brushes for mixing and for larger areas and backgrounds and a few 25 mm and 50 mm brushes for doing colour washes. The long-handled, thinner brushes are the best to use for the actual paint mixing.

Nylon filament brushes are fairly easy to keep clean and should be rinsed out in washing-up liquid from time to time. New brushes should be dipped in white paint before use. This will help them to keep their colour longer.

Children should be encouraged not to leave their brushes standing in water pots but to lie them across palettes or on the table when they are not in use. Brushes left in water will become distorted and will not last so long.

Brush storage

Blocks of wood 5 or 6 cm square drilled with 10 or 12 holes the right size to take the brush handles are the most effective sort of brush stand. Those which hold many more are not so practical in use. Brushes are expensive and need to be cared for if they are to give good service. One of the benefits of making this type of brush stand is that you can immediately see if there are one or two missing at the end of a lesson without having to count them.

Water pots

These can be bought but there are substitutes. It is essential that each child has a water pot, that the water is kept clean and refilled as necessary. Purpose-made, anti-spill water pots with screw tops are alright but can take time to undo and empty. Yogurt cartons are sometimes used but these are unsuitable because they are very easy to knock over. Safer and better are the plastic tubs from margarine or cottage cheese. Half filled these are reasonably accident free, having a wider base.

Rags

Old cloths or stockinette rags are useful as paint rags for wiping brushes, cleaning palettes and general clearing up.

Paper

Just as we try to share our knowledge of other tools and equipment, so we need to help children to know as much as they can about the paper they will be working on. Artists have their own words to describe which way up the paper is to be used. 'Portrait' refers to having the long side vertical (figure 3.3) and 'landscape' to the long side being horizontal (figure 3.4). You need to share these terms with the children so that you and they can use the language of the subject.

Good quality sugar paper is necessary for painting. Ask the children first what they already know about paper. What is it made from and how is it made? Does the process of making it show? Can we tell which is the front? Take black sugar paper as an example. If you compare the two sides of a piece you will find that they are different colours and textures. The darker, smoother side is the front – the side to work on. If you ask them to tear a tiny piece and look at the edge they will be able to see the tiny fibres it is made from. They should not use erasers on sugar paper because the surface will be broken, allowing paint to seep down the fibres, altering the paper's appearance.

Cartridge paper is so called because it was made strong and firm in

3.3   PAPER USED LANDSCAPE WAY UP

3.4   PAPER USED PORTRAIT WAY UP

order to make cartridges for gunpowder. Nowadays it can be bought in different weights, as can other papers and card. The weight of one square metre of paper in grammes is written as GSM, or g/sm, so the larger the number the stronger the paper. This makes a good surface for watercolour as it shows up the transparent quality of the paint.

COLOUR MIXING

In the early years, children need to be introduced to mixing and making their own colours. There is a clear distinction here between the different sorts of painting they will be involved with. They will naturally draw in colours that they like. When the work is concerned with storytelling this is entirely appropriate; but when they are making colours they will need to learn how to make colours which match the resources you have chosen to look at. The process is a gradual one and children need to practise on a regular basis if they are to acquire a 'colour sense', that is to know which colours make other ones and how to make them. Often, when we think about making a painting, we ask the children to make paintings of things, going on a bus or playing on a beach. In these early experiments with colour, 'content free' ideas are best. Simply introduce the paints to the children as a means of finding out about colour. Ask them to use two or three colours to start with and see how many different colours they can make from them. As each colour is made, ask them to try making lines and shapes on the paper, to find out what sort of marks the different brushes will make (figures 3.5 to 3.7). Encourage them to try a range of marks which curl or flow, to make short and long strokes and to see what happens when they add more water.

3.5   COLOUR MIXING
Reception
Powder colour

3.6 COLOUR MIXING
Reception
Powder colour

3.7 COLOUR MIXING
Reception
Powder colour

When the children have had time to explore the paint, give them something simple to observe and work from. Choose something which has predominantly two or three main colours so that they can confidently make those colours. Give them a small piece of the paper they are going to paint on to try out the colours. Then when they have made the range of colours they need, ask them to make a painting of the objects you have chosen. These could be fruit, flowers or even, as shown in figures 3.8 to 3.10, chickens from the school's out-door classroom.

Colour mixing is a basic need in painting and children should be encouraged to learn how to handle both making the colours and being able to control the texture of the paint. The 'primary' colours, those that cannot be made, are yellow, red and blue. 'Secondary' colours are made from two primaries. You will also need white and black which make colours lighter or darker. In a few instances, they change the colour completely; for example, black and yellow make green. The children need to have two reds and two blues to be able to make the full range of colours. They also need to learn the proper names of the colours so that they are able to understand how to use them. The following examples should give an outline for you to use with the children:

Yellow and vermilion (light red) make orange.
Yellow and crimson (purple/red) make a brownish orange.
Yellow and cobalt (light green/blue) make 'grass' green.
Yellow and ultramarine (dark purple/blue) make 'sea' green.
Vermilion and cobalt make brown.
Crimson and ultramarine make purple.

Without these particular colours, the children cannot make all of the colours. Ask them to experiment with two or three at a time and to remember what they used to make a particular colour. They should try out the colours to keep a record of how many they have made (figures 3.11 and 3.12). It is always helpful to have some resources for the children to look at and any things which have a range of secondary colours will give them ample scope – for example, autumn leaves, bread or fruit (figures 3.13 to 3.16).

Black, as mentioned earlier, is best made from the colours you have. This takes patience the first time but the children will find it fascinating. You should practise yourself first, so that you can explain it to them. Mix some yellow on your palette, then add vermilion and ultramarine. The quantities have to be right and you may need to go on adding first one and then the other for some time. If the colour tends to blue add more red, if it is too brown add more blue. It does work and after the first time you will be able to help the children to get it right. Black you have made yourself fits in with the other colours in a painting; ready-made black paint looks artificial. By adding white to your 'home made' black you will find you can create an extensive range of greys, to which you can then add other colours to get a variety of tones, so that you have a bright colour for the foreground and a softer tone for the distance.

3.8 PAINTINGS OF FLOWERS
Year 1
Powder colour

3.9 HENS IN THE OUTDOOR CLASSROOM
Year 1
Powder colour

3.10 HENS IN THE OUTDOOR CLASSROOM
Year 1
Powder colour

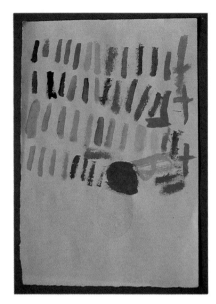

**3.11   COLOUR MIXING
EXPERIMENTS**

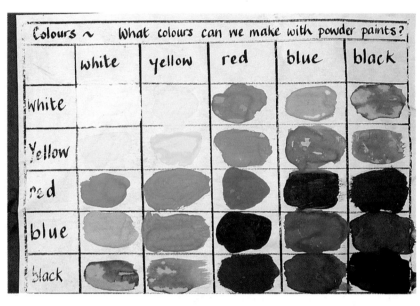

**3.12   COLOUR MIXING
EXPERIMENTS**

As part of our work about harvest, we looked at different kinds of bread.

3.13   COLOUR MATCHING
Year 1
Powder colour

blue + yellow + red = brown

3.14   COLOUR MATCHING
Year 1
Powder colour

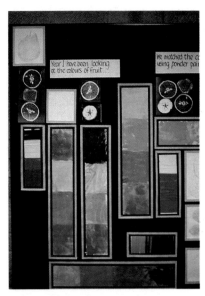

3.15 COLOUR MATCHING
Year I
Powder colour

3.16 COLOUR MATCHING
Year I
Powder colour

PAINTING METHODS

The use of paint provides the best and most flexible medium for exploring colour. It is important as a means of learning vocabulary both generally and specifically in terms of the subject. It is valuable to experience the unique and particular qualities of paint and to foster the understanding, skilful use and manipulation of the medium. Painting is important as a means of personal expression, allowing creative and imaginative use of colour to express ideas and feelings and to explore the visual world.

Children gain self-confidence through the ability to handle and control a substance as complex as paint and by being able to express and communicate ideas through painting. Learning about the way artists, past and present, have used paint can extend the range of possibilities for children in their knowledge and thinking.

Beginning to paint

It must be said that a coloured drawing is not a painting and an appreciation of the difference is important. A careful drawing, that has taken time to do, which is then painted over is not likely to be successful. Children can often resist the request to paint because they feel it would spoil a drawing on which they have spent time. A painting should be tackled in terms of what is possible and appropriate to the medium. Learning about paint is a gradual process, beginning at five and developing in complexity as understanding grows. At the beginning, a clear distinction needs to be made between the use of paint as a medium for drawing with a brush and its use to match and portray real things and ideas.

Unlike a drawing which may have one set of marks across the paper, a painting is built up in layers. Setting out where things are to go in a painting is best done with paint on a brush. Pencil shows through the surface of the paint, whereas paint blends in as the work goes on.

In this example the children made paintings of their favourite teddy bear. The first is clearly still at the symbolic stage and has drawn the teddy with paint (figure 3.17). In the second (figure 3.18), the drawing was made in paint and then worked on to give more information about the texture of the fur. The third (figure 3.19) shows a painting of a bear, where a composition has been made and the whole work has been thought of as a picture in its own right, not simply a copy of the appearance of the bear.

3.17 TEDDY BEAR
Year 2
Powder colour

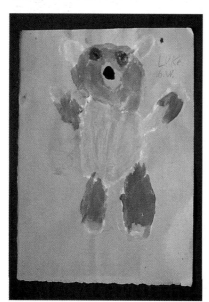

3.18 TEDDY BEAR
Year 2
Powder colour

3.19 TEDDY BEAR
Year 2
Powder colour

Powder colour

Tempera is a word which is nowadays used to describe any non-transparent paint which reflects light from its surface. The texture of paint needs to be explored in the same way that the children experimented with making colours. It can be mixed with the minimum of water, or made very wet and thin. Impasto is a word which means particularly thick and heavy paint and it can be made by adding some PVA glue to the paint. This will also give it a sheen. Impasto is useful for large-scale, or group work as it makes the colours bright and clear (figure 3.20).

A wash can be made from powder colour by making it very watery and thin. It is used for backgrounds or to colour the paper before you start to paint on it. In the example shown in figure 3.21 the sky and grass have been put in as colour washes before the foreground was painted in thicker paint on top.

3.20 LARGE-SCALE GROUP PAINTING
Year 1
Powder colour

3.21 VULTURE
Year 6
Powder colour

3.22 VULTURE
Year 6
Powder colour

In the second example you can compare the thickness of the paint in the previous one with the way it has been used more thinly, to paint the bird first and then add a suitable background. You can see from the direction of the brush strokes that it was done in that order. The project here focused on making a painting of the vulture in its natural habitat, and using the imagination to provide a characteristic background for the bird (figure 3.22).

Water colour

This is essentially a transparent medium where the white of the paper forms the white and light in the painting. In the primary school you may find that white needs to be added for highlights, but the character of watercolour is to use it thinly and as a contrast to the opaque or thicker quality of tempera (figure 3.23). Watercolour paints are suitable for small-scale work where their delicate, clear colours can be used. They are also useful to take out on a visit for making colour notes.

CHOOSING SUBJECTS FOR PAINTING

Using the medium

If the children have not used paints frequently they may need to be introduced to making paintings so that they can concentrate on using the medium and not have to be concerned with choosing and handling subject matter as well. The two examples here outline ways in which the children can work individually, and get used to working with paint.

To make these colour studies you could ask the children to choose and cut out a small piece of a coloured illustration from a magazine. Stick it on to a sheet of paper and begin by mixing the colours in the illustration. Then use the colours to extend those in your picture. In figures 3.24 and 3.25 you can see that they were made into colour landscapes with an horizon, sky and foreground. Any small illustrations can be extended in this way.

In the second example, the children were given small kaleidoscopes – the sort with a marble at the end. They had to look down it and make a painting of the coloured pattern they could see (figures 3.26 and 3.27). It was important that it was secret, because each child had their own pattern, therefore no one needed to compare whose was best! This is important if you need to build confidence.

Working from observation

In painting terms this means working directly from something set up in your room or from colour notes and information collected and brought back into the classroom. The latter has the advantage that paintings can be composed and not just be a recording of an object or scene.

In the example shown in figure 3.28 the children had been out to look at the countryside and had looked at paintings of landscapes by artists like Van Gogh and Cézanne. A painting is essentially about colour and paint and the way they are controlled and used. Paintings are made up of the basic elements of line, tone, shape, form, pattern and texture. So while the children may have been out to look at the landscape, when they come to make a painting it should say more than just what it looked like. In this illustration you can see that the child has tried to show the things he or she enjoyed about the scene. Look at the way the flowers have been arranged to make an interesting pattern, not necessarily drawn as they were. The textures in the sky, corn and foreground all convey feelings of light and air and the tones enhance the mood and atmosphere.

3.23 LANDSCAPE PAINTING
Year 6
Watercolour

3.24 COLOUR LANDSCAPES
Year 3
Powder colour

3.25 COLOUR LANDSCAPES
Year 3
Powder colour

3.26 KALEIDOSCOPE PATTERN
Year 4
Powder colour

3.27 KALEIDOSCOPE PATTERN
Year 4
Powder colour

3.28 LANDSCAPE PAINTING
Year 6
Powder colour

**3.29 PATTERN MADE BY
LOOKING AT A
MAGNIFIED SLIDE OF
RIPPLING WATER**
Year 6
Powder colour

Working from memory or imagination

In working from memory and the imagination we are dealing with the same elements but you need to support the making of the painting through research and visual information. In this example the children had been doing a fiction-based project and had been reading about some of the heroic exploits of lifeboatmen. To help in understanding how to paint water they projected a slide of a lake on to the classroom wall. Using viewfinders, they each selected an area they found interesting and made a painting of the colours they could see (figure 3.29). They also looked at the sky in the same way and then at paintings by artists like Constable and Turner to see how they had handled the same subjects. With this information, they went on to compose and paint their own versions of how they imagined a scene from the book might have been (figure 3.30).

MAKING A PAINTING

The success of any project relies to some extent on the preparation and resourcing. So in planning to make paintings there are several important aspects you need to take into consideration: matching the subject to things of current interest and relevance to the children; having available the right tools and equipment and sufficient space for them to work. As in every activity children will not cope well if they are too cramped and this can affect the quality of their work. If space is limited, use paint with half or a third of the children and a dry colour medium with the others so that you can all do the same work. Rotate the groups on future occasions.

In a similar way to that described in resourcing a drawing activity when the tools and equipment are organised the children need access to reference materials. These need to be in the form of works of art (to support their enquiry into the subject), actual objects to look at (like the slide of water in the previous example) and time to look, talk and plan their work.

The series of illustrations in figures 3.31 to 3.37 shows how one class tackled making their own work using some of J M W Turner's paintings. They began by practising making the colours they would need and then lightly drew in the horizon line and positioned the things that would be in the painting, using soft yellow or a light brown (figures 3.31 and 3.32). Next they painted or put a wash on the large areas of colour to fill the paper with colour (figures 3.33 and 3.34). The next step was to draw again with paint over the top of the background putting in some of the shapes of the buildings or landscape. From there on to the end of the painting they were able to refine colours and add detail (figures 3.35 to 3.37).

Some of the most valuable aspects of learning about painting in the primary school are that children learn about and come to understand colour, to be able to control paint and to use this knowledge to express ideas and feelings. Children love to paint and do it because they enjoy it.

The opportunity to experiment, coupled with sensitive teaching, will enable them to build their skills to match their expectations and their need to produce results which are satisfactory in their own terms. Confidence in the process and in themselves is essential if they are going to gain the benefits of being able to take pleasure in it and communicate through this medium.

3.30 PAINTING OF A LIFEBOAT AT SEA
Year 6
Powder colour

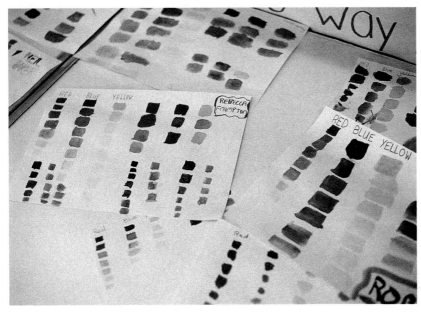

3.31 COLOUR PRACTICE AND LAYOUT
Year 6
Powder colour

3.32 COLOUR PRACTICE
Year 6
Powder colour

3.33 MAKING THE PAINTINGS
Year 6
Powder colour

3.34 MAKING THE PAINTINGS
Year 6
Powder colour

3.35 PAINTING OF LANDSCAPE
Year 6
Powder colour

3.36 PAINTING OF LANDSCAPE
Year 6
Powder colour

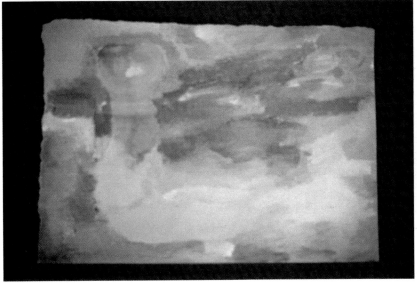

3.37 PAINTING OF LANDSCAPE
Year 6
Powder colour

4 Two-dimensional design

4.1 CHILDREN MAKING A BLOCK PRINT
Years 5 and 6
Card block, water-based printing inks

4.2 CHILDREN MAKING A BLOCK PRINT
Years 5 and 6
Card block, water-based printing inks

TWO-DIMENSIONAL DESIGN IN CONTEXT

So far we have looked at the way children learn about the world through seeing it in terms of drawing and painting but there are many other ways of recording, interpreting and affecting our environment. Throughout history people have been changing the world to make it easier to manage to get food and to live more comfortably. Designers and craftspeople have changed the design of things to make them more effective or easier to use. To be able to do this they have had to understand the processes by which things are made. Children need to learn about that world, to know how things are made and how they have evolved over time. They need to learn about these processes in the primary school and to understand the particular skills that are associated with the way that changes are made. They need your help to learn about making prints and textiles and being able to operate a computer so that later on they have the basic skills, vocabulary and knowledge to cope with more advanced work.

There are many books on individual subject skills and instructions on how to do things. What you need to know is how to place those skills in context for the children. You also need to know something about the various types of craft involved and have some knowledge of the processes so that you can see where what you teach fits into the wider world of each subject area. So here we are going to look at the various aspects of design that you need to know about in order to be able to give the children a breadth of experience and an opportunity to learn about some of the processes.

PRINT MAKING

There are many things involved with these processes that seem like magic. When children make their first print it should be an exciting experience as well as one which broadens their knowledge (see figures 4.1 to 4.3). Making a print means that instead of creating one piece of work at a time you can produce many prints from the same original. There are so many different forms of printing and we are so familiar with printed products that it is easy to forget that so much is made by sophisticated versions of this simple process. This book is an example of a high order of typography and the colour printing process. Newspapers and magazines are printed in their millions and every cereal packet we buy is an example of sophisticated commercial printing.

At the opposite end of the spectrum, artists have used a variety of print-making processes to do their own work. The prints produced can be used for a variety of purposes, either as works of art in their own right to be framed and viewed like paintings or as book illustrations. Artists throughout history have often employed more than one method of making their work and there are many who are as well known for their print making as for their drawing or painting. Try to find some illustrations of prints made by well-known artists when you introduce

4.3 CHILDREN MAKING A BLOCK PRINT
Years 5 and 6
Card block, water-based printing inks

each new print-making process to the children. As each print is made from a block or plate it is numbered. The numbers are written like a fraction. The number on top of the line indicates the order in which it was made and the number below the line tells how many prints are to be made. Fine art prints are made in limited editions and it depends on the type of block used how many good prints can be made from it.

Printing methods

Etching and engraving are methods of cutting into a surface. In etching, the plate is covered with wax and a line is drawn in with a sharp point. Then it is put in an acid bath. The acid eats into the metal where the lines have been drawn through the wax. The artist controls how deep the lines are by how long the plate stays in the acid. Rembrandt worked mainly with this method to make his prints.

Engraving is different in that the lines are cut directly into the plate. In both these methods the print comes from the ink which is left in the cut lines of the plate, not from the surface of the block.

Potato cuts, wood cuts and lino cuts are also direct cutting methods. Here the surface of the block is printed, not the cutaway areas. Wood cuts are probably the oldest form, dating back to at least the sixth century AD when they were used for printing textiles. Later they appear as book illustrations. Try to find some examples of work by Thomas Bewick. Wood cuts were also used extensively by the Japanese. Look at the work of Torii Kiyohiro in the Resource Pack (no. 14). Lino cutting was a much later invention and was used earlier this century by artists like Matisse and Picasso. In primary schools we use specially prepared polystyrene blocks to draw into as they are much quicker and safer to

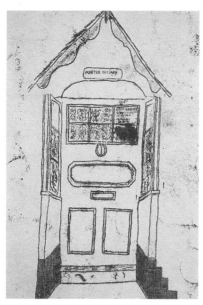

4.4   MONO PRINT
Year 6
Water-based printing inks

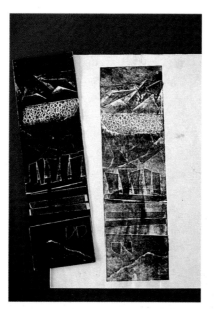

4.5   CARD BLOCK AND PRINT
Year 5
Wallpaper and card block and print

4.6   WALLPAPER BLOCK PRINT
Year 5
Water-based printing inks

use than lino. They produce excellent results through the same process.

Lithography, which was invented in the 18th century, has been used by many artists including William Blake, Toulouse-Lautrec, Matisse and Picasso. In this process an image is drawn on a specially prepared piece of stone or metal using a greasy paint or crayon. Acid is used to 'etch' away the background and the ink is put on to the plate (the stone or metal) and a print taken. There is no equivalent process which is commonly used in school but making a mono print has some of the same characteristics. To do this you spread out the printing ink on a suitable surface like plate glass or smooth and flat formica, draw the design into the ink and take a print directly from the surface. This method only really produces one print from the drawing but it can be an effective method to use with children because it is quick, simple and allows them to see how the process works (figure 4.4).

Collage prints are different from the other processes because the block is built up rather than cut away. They are made by inking the surface of a collage and taking a print from it. This method is suitable for primary school work because it is the most flexible. Children can make their own blocks either from cut and torn paper and card or they can use objects to stick on to a card background and print from that (see figures 4.5 to 4.7). The only restriction is that the block should not be too uneven or too high because that would make it difficult to print.

Silkscreen printing was originally a commercial process which began to be used by artists in the 1930s as it was cheaper than the more traditional materials. The method requires a wooden frame covered in a fine mesh, either organdie or (more cheaply) very fine curtain net. Real silk ceased to be used when it became so expensive. To make a design on the net either block out part of it with a special sort of glue or, more usually for school use, tear or cut out a paper stencil and put the screen over it (figures 4.8 and 4.9). Ink is then forced through the net on to a surface which can be either paper or fabric, though you can make prints on many surfaces including ceramics.

4.8   OWL SCREEN PRINT
Year 2
Wallpaper paste and readymix

4.9   SCREEN PRINTS
Year 6
Oil-based inks

**4.7   CUT-OUT CARD
BLOCK PRINT**
Year 6
Water-based printing inks

Making prints in Key Stage 1

With small children tactile experiences are important. They need to use their hands to find out how things feel and to learn more about themselves. Begin by asking the children to make hand prints using finger paints. Get them to develop this by using fingers to make patterns and designs on paper. You will need to talk with them about several things: first, that when they make this sort of print the object is reversed on the paper it comes out the other way round; and then about how they can affect the results by changing the thickness of the paint or ink they are using. Texture is very important in printing and children need to be sensitive to the quality of the marks that are made in both substances.

The next step is to find a variety of things to print with, like heavy card and corrugated cardboard used flat and on edge, cotton reels, shells and anything with a textured surface. Again it is important for the children to begin by experimenting with making the prints. When they can do this well, they can begin to use the method to represent other things. In the illustrations (figures 4.10 and 4.11) the children had been looking at some flower paintings and at the wild flowers growing in their own school grounds. They tried out all sorts of objects to find which made the most suitable marks to represent the flowers.

Vegetable and potato prints are the next types of process to explore. One way is to cut different sorts of fruit and vegetables in half and print them either with their own moisture (beetroot works well here), or roll out some ink and lightly press the vegetables or fruit into it and then print them. Alternatively, using a swede or potato the children can cut them in half and carve a pattern or design in the flat surface. Here again they could print them using paint or inks. It is important to encourage them to make patterns and designs by overprinting the blocks and using different colours to build up a design.

Mono prints can be made simply in this Key Stage by introducing ink to the children if they have used paint to make their prints up to this point. They need to try rolling the ink out well. That is, they need to roll it on a flat surface of metal, formica or the tabletop until it is smooth and develops a velvety texture. They can use one or more colours but they must be rolled out evenly. Then they have to draw into the ink using any tool capable of making a strong mark in the ink. They should try to have some clear patches as well as a variety of different lines and patterns. Then paper is put over the print and gently smoothed down on to the ink by hand, taking care not to move it or it will smudge. Next comes the exciting experience of peeling the paper off the print. In common with most printing methods it will come out in reverse. Remember: if you want to have an idea what the print will look like while you are still in the drawing stage you can use a mirror to help you to see it back to front. This is especially useful if lettering is involved.

4.10 **PRINTS FROM CARD AND SPONGES**
Year I
Readymix paint

Printing in Key Stage 2

Of the methods used in the previous section, mono prints work equally well with older children who will be able to make more detailed use of the process. The other methods they should become familiar with are collage prints, poly or press print and silk screen. Lino cutting presents several problems, including finding a method of keeping it warm enough so that it is possible to cut into it and hoping the children will avoid cutting their fingers. The other printing processes included here cover all you will need to do with the children in their primary years.

Design takes on a far more important role here because with all the methods except mono printing the block has to be made first and its final design can only be seen with the aid of a mirror. The options at this stage are to work from observation or the imagination; in either case drawings need to be made to give an opportunity for the design to be refined and modified to suit the process. For example, if the children have been making drawings of local houses looking at the textures of the building materials they might need to work out a scale to work to so that all the prints are approximately the same size. Then a final print could be like a frieze, recreating a street scene from all of the prints.

Collage print making is the most versatile method for this age group. The blocks can be made simply from torn or cut textured wallpapers and thin card and stuck firmly on to a card backing. Allow the glue to dry before attempting to print. As well as sticking paper and card on to the block, fine details can also be drawn with a biro into the surface allowing fine patterns and details to be made.

Specially made polystyrene sheets are obtainable from major art materials manufacturers. They are an excellent substitute for lino and can be used in a similar way. The surface does not need to be cut away, just

4.11 **PRINTS FROM CARD AND SPONGES**
Year I
Readymix paint

4.12 DESIGN SHEETS
Year 6
Biro

drawn on to with a firm point. After a first drawing has been made and printed, the block can be washed and more drawing can be added. This time print the block in another colour; and so on until the design is completed.

Silk screen as a process needs perhaps more preparation time but just as much thought must go into the design. In this example, the children had researched their motifs from books and photographs taken in the locality and developed a repeat design for printing (figures 4.12 to 4.14). As well as making prints on paper, this method is very good for printing on fabrics as we know from the vast variety of printed t-shirts on sale. With the much improved dyes available, this is a practical option for printing your own fabrics.

4.13 SCREEN PRINT
Year 6
Screen printing inks

4.14 SCREEN PRINT
Year 6
Screen printing inks

TEXTILES

In print making the different processes need to be introduced one after the other because they depend on increasingly complex operations and use of materials. It is appropriate to start with the simpler hand and card prints and then, when print-making principles have been understood, move on to card block and screenprint making. In work in fabrics and textiles the structure is different. The four different areas of textiles can all be tackled in **Key Stage 1** and built on in **Key Stage 2** with the children gradually becoming more competent in skill and understanding. A five-year-old can make a simple weaving in coloured paper or threads, a batik or a print on fabric, and in Year 1 or 2 you may begin some stitching and appliqué. Your role is to introduce the various skills so that the children enjoy the processes and are excited by the possibilities. Each area becomes more complex as the children become more accomplished. As they appreciate ways of making or printing fabrics they will see the need to plan and design their work appropriately. Here we are going to look at each of the four major areas of textiles and outline ways of planning and structuring a course through **Key Stages 1 and 2** They are not taken here in order of importance. All textiles skills complement each other and enhance our understanding of the ways in which clothing, furnishing fabrics and decorative articles are made.

Although it is not appropriate to describe it in detail here, it is always useful to look at the way that the basic raw materials are produced. The Humanities offer opportunities for exploring the ways in which cotton, silk, linen, wool and synthetic fibres are produced.

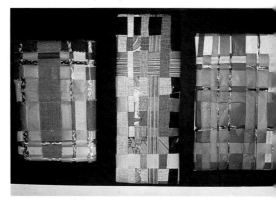

4.15 PAPER WEAVING
Year 2
Coloured and shiny papers

Weaving

First the children must be given the opportunity to find out how fabrics are made by weaving one thread over and under another. Weaving strips of paper makes the process clear. Choose a theme which is simple and clear in colour terms. For example, like the weavings in the Indian project in *Principles and Practice*, the colours you can see from your room or the colours they are wearing (figure 4.15).

Having understood the process, children next need to know about the quality, colour and texture of threads and yarns. Learning about this can take many forms. The children need to spend time discussing the 'feel' of cottons, wools and synthetics using words like thickness, roughness, smoothness and talking about the mixture of colours in a selection of threads and yarns (figure 4.16). It is important to take time over learning about the qualities of the materials so that the children can really learn what a wonderful variety of materials there are to use. They should also be learning the language appropriate to the subject. A loom describes the framework on which the weaving is made. 'Warp' is the word for the collection of threads which run lengthwise in the fabric. They need to be plain, strong threads and can range in thickness from cotton to fine string. The word 'weft' describes the coloured and textured threads which are woven over and under the warp to form the weaving.

4.16 CHILDREN SORTING YARNS AND THREADS

Yarn wrappings

To introduce this aspect of learning about fabrics you need to have a large collection of different threads and yarns for them to choose from. These can be collected from local sources such as stores or sales and you can encourage the children to help by asking families to donate any old balls of wool or threads that they have at home. Having the materials available, you need to introduce a stimulus or focus for the work. Choose something which has relevance for the children. In other subjects they may be looking at particular areas of the Humanities, Science or Language, or it may be that they are illustrating the colours used in a work of art (figures 4.17 and 4.18). Choose a subject which involves colour and texture and ask them to think about the colours which best express the feeling or atmosphere of the focus they have chosen. Ask them to select from the threads and yarns available those colours and textures which best tell how they see their picture and wrap the yarns to show the particular order of colours in their chosen subject (figure 4.19).

4.17 YARN WRAPPINGS USING WORKS OF ART
Year 6
Coloured yarns

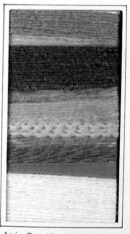

Craig Caithness
Klimt : The Swamp

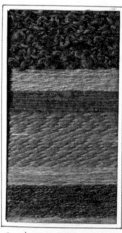

Mia Bartlett
Klimt : Quiet Pond N°5

A view of the cliff at Branscombe

Tessa Lambert

4.19 YARN WRAPPING, LANDSCAPE
Year 6
Coloured yarns

Victoria Stipwill
Van Gogh : Olive Trees in a Mountain Landscape

Ashley Counter
Van Gogh : Wheat Field Under Clouded Skies

4.18 YARN WRAPPINGS USING WORKS OF ART
Year 6
Coloured yarns

4.20 WEAVING FRAMES

4.21 IMPROVISED LOOMS

Cardboard and wood-framed looms

These may well be familiar from the commercially produced variety but children can make their own to fit the size and proportion of the subject they want to work on (figure 4.20). The warp has to be carefully and precisely wrapped around a piece of card or strawboard, or over the wooden frame, and secured firmly at the back. This is suitable for weaving straight into with the minimum of planning. Select colours and threads to fit any subject (like the yarn wrappings), to show times of day, the seasons or to reflect different moods. Or you may wish to make tapestry weavings, like the ones described in the next section, by slipping the drawing under the warp and matching colours to the design.

Improvised looms

These include looms made from dowel rods or small branches with weights hung on them to keep the warp taut. The two illustrated here are different sizes and show what a variety of forms you can choose from to suit your circumstances (figures 4.21 and 4.22). The children can draw and colour their designs on paper and put these behind the warp so that they can follow it like a pattern, choosing the colours and textures of yarns and threads to match the design. The weavings can be made equally well individually or in groups to suit the size of the design. This offers the opportunity to undertake both small- and large-scale work. Artists in residence are mentioned in *Understanding in Art* but it is important, too, to have craftspeople in residence to do their own work and explain the processes they use to the children (figures 4.23 and 4.24). It can be an exciting start to a project to have a visit from someone who works full-time and earns their living by their skills in a particular craft area. It lends credibility to the process by showing it in a wider context than purely as a school-based activity.

A weaving project

This project looked at the way children could use a fiction-based theme, find relevant first-hand material to study and whichever craft area they chose, be able to relate the things they found into designs and ideas for

4.22 IMPROVISED LOOMS

4.23 TAPESTRY WEAVING, CRAFTSPERSON IN RESIDENCE

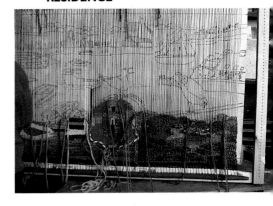

different craft areas. In this example the children were doing a fiction-based project. They were reading *Carrie's War*, enjoyed the story and chose to use it as a starting point for a variety of pieces of work, one of which involved making a weaving. Taking the passage about the druid's grove they began by making careful drawings to explain the complicated patterns and lines on large pieces of wood (figure 4.25). Next they used a viewfinder to 'keyhole' a section of the drawing they found most interesting and made a larger version of this. They paid particular attention to the tones and textures on the log (figure 4.26). Then, using the information they had gained, they designed and made a weaving which, for them, reflected something about the original story (figure 4.27).

Fabric printing

This aspect of work belongs here but as it is also heavily dependent on methods of making the prints the process was described in the section on print making. As before, you need an initial stimulus and this can be based on a whole range of subjects from natural and made objects, to festivals and project work. Using drawing to design a block or template, the children can try out and practise printing on paper. Cut potatoes and vegetables, blocks made from found objects, or the silk screen process can all be used. Many fabrics are available from school suppliers or you can use old sheets or old fabrics you may have. If you are experimenting and using paint to print with, any fabric will do. If, however, you want to use dyes, check the instructions carefully and always use cotton or fabrics made from natural fibres. Most dyes will not work on synthetic fabrics. New ranges of dyes, fabric crayons and paints, all of which can be 'fixed' (i.e. made permanent and washable) are being developed and should be available for school use.

**4.24 TAPESTRY WEAVING,
CRAFTSPERSON IN
RESIDENCE**

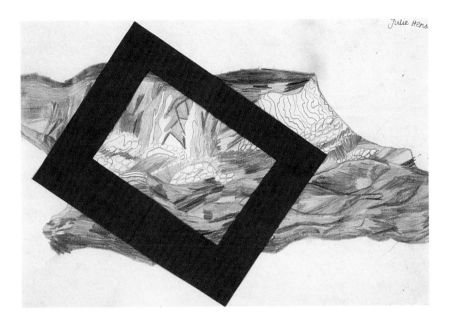

Julie Hens.

4.25 DRAWING WITH 'KEYHOLE' USING A VIEWFINDER
Year 5
Pencil

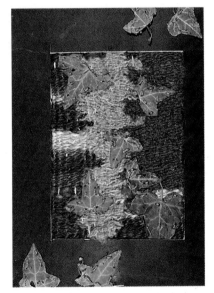

4.26 ENLARGING A DRAWING
Year 5
Chalk and charcoal

4.27 TAPESTRY WEAVING
Year 5
Coloured yarns and ivy

In planning a course in fabric printing you would need to introduce vegetables and found objects using paint on small pieces of fabric. Ask the children to practise and experiment with printing and over printing to build up patterns. After the initial experience, they could go on to learning about different ways of making and using blocks and screens to produce fabrics for making cushions, curtains or hangings. Computers have an important role here: some programs make it possible to draw a design, select an area of it to enlarge, show it in, for example, brick, half drop or quarter drop repeats, and then change the colours through a wide range of choices. This makes it easy to choose a preferred design and use it to make the block or screen.

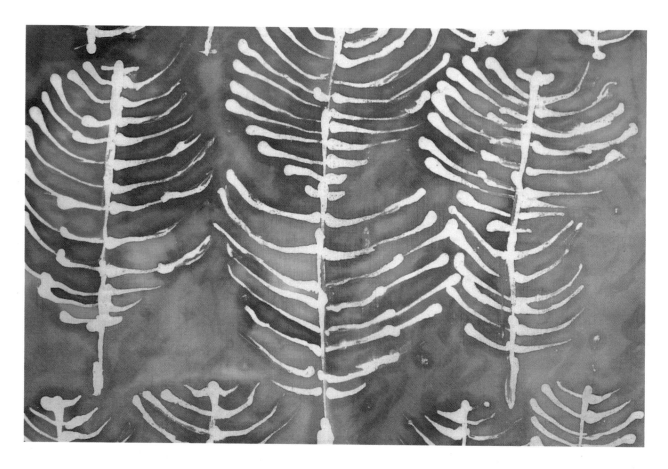

**4.28 BATIK BASED ON LEAF
FORMS**
Year 6

**4.29 OBSERVATION DRAWING
OF PLANTS**
Year 5/6

Ink and watercolour

Batik

Batik is a resist process. This means that the fabric you are going to dye
has a coating of wax on parts of it and these remain undyed. Specially
designed wax kettles which are small and compact are available. One or
two of these should enable you to set up a batik area where children can
go, one at a time, to make their batiks. With this process health and
safety considerations are particularly important. It needs organising so
that the children understand the procedure and are working where you
can see them. Lines of wax are drawn with a Tjanting tool, a small brass
cup with a spout which allows wax to dribble gently on to the fabric. Or
you can use a brush, but this is less successful because it can clog as the
wax cools. If using wax is a problem, there is an alternative resist called
Gutta, which is painted on to the fabric in the same way, and is available
through schools suppliers.

Next, you need a frame over which the fabric can be stretched, so
that it is held out of contact with the table surface. Again, fine cotton or
fabric made of natural fibres needs to be used, in order to take the dye.
The process from there on is one of dying, adding more wax and
redying with a darker colour each time. The dyes should be painted on
with a brush.

The process depends so largely on the equipment that it was necessary to outline what was involved because the products that are made
have highly individual qualities. Fine details are difficult to produce – the

wax or Gutta makes lines and areas of colour rather than precise drawings of things. In the early years, any observation work the children have done can be used as a starting point for making a picture on fabric. Later on, when they understand the process and can use it confidently, patterns based on natural or made objects are appropriate (figure 4.28).

Batiks can also be used, by older children, as part of a more complicated process involving other skills. The starting point for this example was the need to produce a calendar. This process was chosen as it would be colourful, decorative and use several techniques the children were ready to learn. Drawings of seasonal plants were made and used as the basis for a batik (figure 4.29). When that had been made, the children went on to add drawn lines and stitched details in metallic threads (figure 4.30).

The second example uses batik combined with quilting. In their study of the Tudors the children had been interested in contemporary paintings and miniatures showing the rich clothes and jewels that were worn. They were able to plan a piece of work in which they used the batik method to dye the fabric, add the padding and use stitches to quilt the work (figures 4.31 and 4.32).

4.30 CALENDARS
Year 5/6
Batik and embroidery

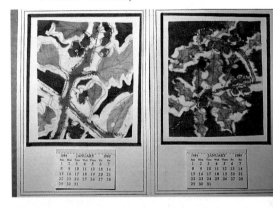

4.32 HENRY VIII
Year 5
Quilted batik

Nicholas Hilliard was a famous Tudor liminer or painter of miniatures

We drew miniatures of the wives of Henry VIII. We enlarged them to add colour and wrote poems with the title "Remember Me."

4.31 DESIGN FOR QUILTED BATIK
Year 5

4.33 SEWING A COLLAGE

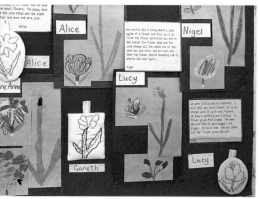

**4.34 OBSERVATION WORK
LEADING TO QUILTED
PICTURES**
Year 4

4.35 COLLAGE
Year 5
Stitched felt

Collage and embroidery

In this section we look at using, rather than making, fabrics. Collage employs all those skills of choosing, matching, and making a design, cutting, placing and joining with glue and stitches. In **Key Stage I** children need to have an opportunity to sort and select threads, yarns and fabrics and use them for picture making because they offer texture as well as colour. They can learn the skills of cutting fabric and sticking down with glue. Later on, when they are introduced to stitching, they can plan and design more complicated pictures to represent things and to tell stories (figure 4.33). They can use this method of fixing things in place. Subject matter here, as before, should be based on first-hand observation or experiences and displays of the work should show the source material as well as the finished product (figure 4.34).

Working from the natural world, the collage and stitched pictures in this example were based on a collection of wild flowers the children had made. To make these you would ask the children to draw flowers, looking carefully at the shapes of leaves and petals; then selecting felts, they would cut them out and stitch them into place using a variety of stitches. It would be appropriate for you to teach the stitches that children felt were most suitable for their designs. You would do this by looking at the drawings they made and asking them to find stitches which were most like the qualities of line and pattern in the drawing (figures 4.35 and 4.36).

As the children become more skilful and know more stitches they can use the technique to represent things more accurately (figures 4.37 and 4.38).

In the last example the drawings of landscapes were made as a starting point for a number of crafts. The whole group shared in looking at and talking about how to carry out further work. Some made landscapes in clay, some used paint and some made embroidery pictures, based on the original drawings (figure 4.39).

USING COMPUTERS IN TWO-DIMENSIONAL DESIGN

We have looked at the way in which computers can aid design in textiles. They have changed the process where an artist had to spend many hours trying out different colours and repeats in a design (figure 4.40). They have also revolutionised the way that graphics are taught. Lettering has become so professional with the aid of desk-top publishing packages (see figure 4.41) that there is no longer any need for the conventional, laborious ways of producing printed information. Instead, the children can concentrate on the design aspects of each craft. The possibilities are virtually endless. Children need to have computer skills and you should encourage them to explore ways of drawing and experimenting around themes and topics in all aspects of art and design (figure 4.42).

Text and drawing combined

Careful drawing, based on observation, can be used to illustrate fiction, writing and poetry. Because the two can be designed and printed together they make a more coherent piece of work and children can develop the designing skills in a way which looks 'professional' (figures 4.43 and 4.44). It is important that they are pleased with the end result.

4.36 COLLAGE
Year 5
Stitched felt

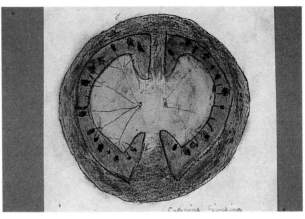

4.37 DESIGN FOR EMBROIDERY
Year 6
Crayon and watercolour

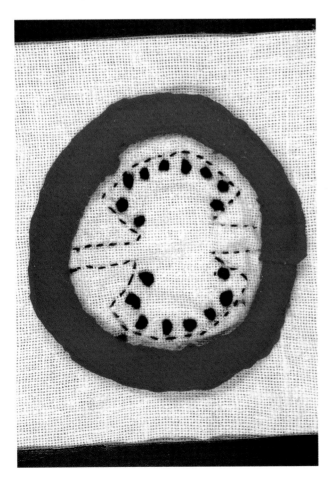

4.39 EMBROIDERY WITH DESIGN DRAWING
Year 6

4.38 EMBROIDERY
Year 6
Fabric and threads

**4.40 COMPUTER-DRAWN
DESIGNS FOR
A MENU CARD**
Year 2

**4.41 COMPUTER-DRAWN
DESIGNS FOR
A MENU CARD**
Year 2

4.42 USING THE COMPUTER

**4.43 BOOK DESIGN WITH
TEXT AND
ILLUSTRATIONS**
Year 5

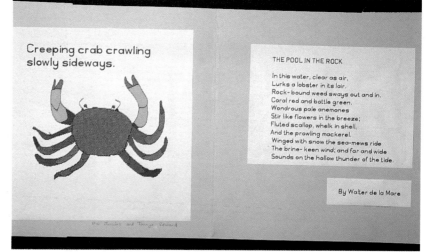

Creeping crab crawling
slowly sideways.

THE POOL IN THE ROCK

In this water, clear as air,
Lurks a lobster in its lair.
Rock-bound weed sways out and in.
Coral red and bottle green,
Wondrous pale anemones
Stir like flowers in the breeze;
Fluted scallop, whelk in shell,
And the prowling mackerel.
Winged with snow the sea-mews ride
The brine-keen wind; and far and wide
Sounds on the hollow thunder of the tide.

By Walter de la Mare

**4.44 BOOK DESIGN WITH
TEXT AND
ILLUSTRATIONS**
Year 5

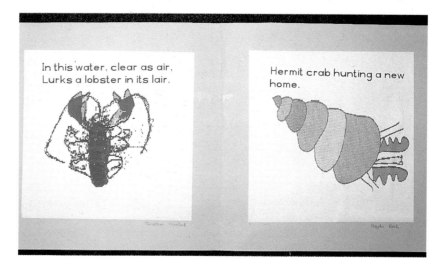

In this water, clear as air,
Lurks a lobster in its lair.

Hermit crab hunting a new
home.

Stamp design

In this example the children were designing stamps as part of a project on flight. They were asked to look at existing stamps and then to choose a subject they thought suitable. After making initial drawings, the designs were transferred to the computer and modified to make them easily recognisable on a small scale. The children experimented with different colours and chose the one they thought most effective (figure 4.45). Repeats are easily done but managing the perforation drawing took time to resolve – the zigzags have to meet (figure 4.46).

Lettering

Learning about lettering and hand-writing will work best in the form of an investigation and appraisal of existing lettering in our surroundings. You could begin by asking the children to collect examples of lettering, sorting them into categories and then discussing how effective, clear, attractive or legible they might be. Then they could design their own for a purpose: for example, hospital directions, road signs or lettering for shopfronts. You could handle handwriting in a similar way, getting children to ask friends and family for samples and then assessing their legibility, attractiveness and character.

4.45 STAMP DESIGNS
Year 5

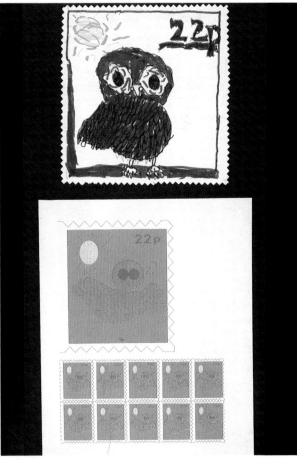

4.46 STAMP DESIGNS
Year 5

5 Three-dimensional design

5.1 OBSERVATION WORK, LOOKING AT FRUIT AND VEGETABLES

5.2 READY FOR THE PLAY

THREE-DIMENSIONAL DESIGN IN CONTEXT

This is an important area of activity for children because it offers opportunities for them to work with a less familiar range of materials than paper and paint and to learn how to solve problems in new ways.

In their survey of schools recently HMI found little interest in three-dimensional work and not much evidence of good and exciting practice. We need to appreciate why it is important and then look at ways in which we can organise and resource this area of experience effectively.

Three-dimensional craft work is important because it is part of the past, to be learned from, and it offers opportunities for children to develop unique skills. In our study of history we look at how people in the past painted and drew on cave walls and how gradually processes and materials have become refined. We should be equally aware of the rich heritage we share in the world of sculpture, ceramics, construction and architecture. Much of the work in the past has been functional and we need to begin by looking at examples of different sorts of work to find out what was made and why. For example, have a look at the pair of wooden doors made by the people of Yoruba in the Resource Pack (no. 8) to see how they were able to make functional things so interesting.

Experience in three-dimensional work can help children to understand more about their world but this is not the most important reason for involving ourselves in it. In handling materials, we and the children enter a new world of experience (figure 5.1). Each of the processes has individual characteristics and needs different skills in understanding and handling. Just as some children are good at drawing or painting, others will find they have natural ability to handle other materials and they must be given that opportunity. However, your attitude will determine the success of the work. If the children feel that these are activities you want them to do while you are occupied with something else the 'body language' will tell them you do not think it is important. You need to handle the materials yourself so that you can help and advise, offer suggestions and know how to cope if things come apart.

You need the confidence to handle three-dimensional work just as they need your support to gain access to all these valuable experiences (figure 5.2). Some of the children will have preferences, so in your own school you will have teachers who prefer one craft area to another and may indeed have some specialist knowledge they can share. In any one year, there is only time for one or possibly two craft areas to be covered in reasonable depth. You need to look at your own circumstances and plan to do one main craft with each year group, arranging this to match with those teachers who have some knowledge of and liking for that craft area.

When we looked at painting we recognised that it would be best to work in groups and avoid children having to wait to clean palettes or refill water pots. In craft work you can organise your class in the same way. The important thing is to work from the resources, experience or stimulus with the whole class. Initial organisation must be planned. Then when the children are used to the routine, work can proceed smoothly. When using clay or construction materials try to set aside a craft area, near a sink if possible. All the children can listen to the same input and they can all share the discussion and ask questions. Then half or a third of them can work with dry colour, pastels or crayons, and some with pencil, biro or fibre tip. It does take initial organisation but the children should certainly be able to respond and understand that as groups move round they will be able to take part in many more activities (figure 5.3). This type of organisation is better than an 'arts' circus because the work is seen as part of the essential work of the group, not as a fringe activity.

The sort of experiences that children need include work with 'plastic' materials like playdough, plasticine and clay, 'rigid' materials like soap, block salt, cheese hard clay and soft stone for carving and construction materials like newspapers, card, wire, modroc, plaster, wood and plastics. This list is intended to outline the options available as you will certainly not do them all. The National Curriculum asks for children to plan and make three-dimensional work and structures for a variety of purposes and using various materials. You can choose what will best suit your situation and the expertise within your school from the variety of craftwork discussed in the following chapter.

In the same way that we have looked at the work of other artists to inform and enhance our own work, you will need to collect illustrations of three-dimensional work made by artists and craftworkers past and present. If you can classify postcards and pictures into various categories – for example, sculpture, ceramics, constructions and carving – the children will begin to distinguish how they were made and what materials and processes were used. Familiarity will help them to distinguish as easily between work in clay, wood, metal or plastics as we would expect them to do between pencil, pen and ink, crayons and paint. This may seem too simple an aim but it is one which, at present, many children could not achieve.

5.3 MAKING HOUSES IN CLAY

Drawing is not a prerequisite of work in three dimensions. It may take the form of working directly into the material and building as you go. But it is useful to collect work by sculptors like Henry Moore, with his drawings of sheep and people sleeping in the air-raid shelters in the Second World War, Dame Elizabeth Frink with designs for her bird, animal and human sculptures and Barbara Hepworth with drawings for her abstract carvings and bronzes.

All of these will help to put the world of three-dimensional design in context for the children.

USING PLASTIC MATERIALS

These include playdough, plasticine and clay. As with two-dimensional design, there are many instructional books which explain how to do the different processes. What you need to know is how important each area of experience is in relation to others and how to use it with children. Every teacher of Reception and Year 1 will appreciate the importance of playdough to the children. Handling the dough enables them to find out what happens when you squeeze, press and mould it. No other activities apart from dough, plasticine and clay give the same opportunities for practising and refining motor skills. This is the only area where we place importance on what children can do with their hands. It is a very important activity and one which it is easy to ignore.

Playdough

As with any material new to the children, they need time to experiment and find out what it will do. It could be that for some it is an extension of playing with food, pushing and handling it and seeing how far they can make it spread. When they have had time to experiment, they can go on to make things. Children's recall of what foods look like is stronger, perhaps, than any other visual memory and they will be able to make fruit, vegetables and meals well. Developing out of this you can lead them on to materials which have wider possibilities.

Plasticine

As a modelling material plasticine has limitations. It is not as flexible as clay but it does have the advantage of in-built colour and is good for small-scale work. In the same way that David Hockney made using coloured pencils more popular, the work done by Nick Clark in using plasticine to make the parrots, pandas, cats and beagles for short films and television advertising commercials shows just what can be achieved.

Clay work

Clay, as a material, is the most flexible medium for modelling. When you introduce it to children, begin with buff or grey. Red clay can be lovely to use but it stains hands and some children find this difficult to cope with in the initial stages. Also before they have handled clay for the first time,

5.4   OBSERVATION WORK
Year 3
Clay, paint and varnish

5.5   HORSE CHESTNUTS
Year 4
Clay and glaze

**5.6   WORKING FROM
OBSERVATION**
Year 5
Clay

5.7   THE PICNIC
Year 1
Clay and glaze

take a small amount out of the bin and roll and squeeze it while you explain what the children will be doing. By the time they actually get their clay the children should be keen to handle it for themselves and no one will find the texture off putting. Again, the difference between a teacher who is keen to be involved and one who stands back will be reflected in the success of the children's work and attitude to the subject.

Three-dimensional work is often easier for children to do because the resources they will be working from are themselves three dimensional. Having played and experimented with the clay, children should begin with some observational work. You can choose from a wide range of small familiar objects for them to make. It will be obvious that it is easier to make pebbles, horse chestnuts or fruit in the round, just as they appear, than to try to draw them on a flat surface – at least many children will find it so (figures 5.4 to 5.6).

In order to learn the skills of joining, rolling out tiles, using slip (semi-liquid material used for cementing, coating or decorating pottery) and decorating in context, you need to plan a series of activities based on topics or other areas of study. This means that the children have a real purpose in making, they are not just learning skills in isolation.

We will look at three major areas that you might choose on which to base some work. They are interchangeable with many others. Figures play a large part in our lives and are important as models for all kinds of work in art and craft. In both Key Stages we can see these different ways of tackling the subject (figures 5.7 to 5.9). Although each child will make their own figure, it is always more interesting if they fit into an overall group. They can be displayed together and are still separate for the children to take home (figure 5.10). Nativity groups and figures made to illustrate other festivals and celebrations are an exciting focus for this work (figures 5.11 and 5.12).

5.8 VIOLINISTS
Year 2
Biscuit fired clay

5.9 VIOLINISTS
Year 2
Biscuit fired clay

5.10 THE CRICKET MATCH
Year 6
Biscuit fired clay

5.12 NATIVITY FIGURES
Year 4/5
Clay and glaze

5.11 NATIVITY FIGURES
Year 4/5
Clay and glaze

5.13 PANEL, BASED ON PLANT FORM
Year 3
Clay and glaze

Although printing into clay with found objects can be a good experience, there needs to be a way of going beyond this to something design based. In these examples there are tiles, both open and solid, making a panel to illustrate different sorts of plants (figure 5.13), a design based on a Roman tile from a study of the Romans (figure 5.14) and an Aztec God, made by a group of children to show characteristic headgear and jewels (figure 5.15).

Landscape is another familiar focus and can be tackled in several ways in clay. One example shows how tiles can be rolled out and built together to form a box, where the landscape is modelled on the front of each tile (figures 5.16 and 5.17). In another example tiles have again been used but they have been moulded to form a base on which the landscape can be modelled. This involves intricate work and gives children the opportunity to produce something entirely personal, to make it the way they want within an overall framework (figures 5.18 to 5.21).

Works of art are another valuable starting point, especially when they can be combined with looking at real things. In the first of two examples, the children were staying at a residential centre and were using works of

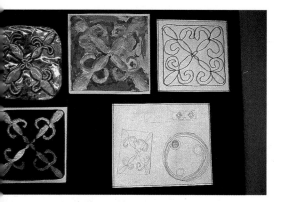

5.14 DESIGN BASED ON A ROMAN TILE
Year 5
Mixed media

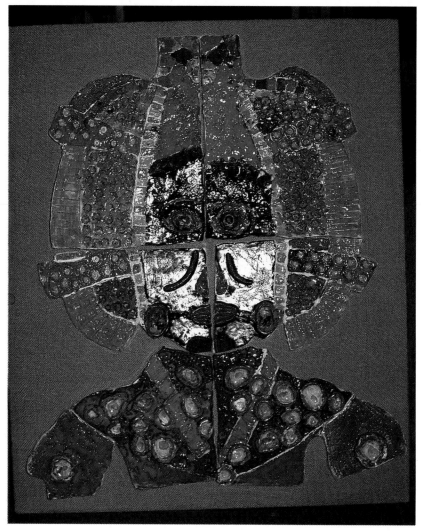

5.15 AZTEC GOD
Year 5
Clay, glaze and glass insets

5.16 LANDSCAPES
Year 6
Clay and glaze

5.17 LANDSCAPE
Year 6
Clay and glaze

5.18 LANDSCAPE MODELLING
Year 6
Clay

5.19 LANDSCAPE MODELLING
Year 6
Clay

5.20 LANDSCAPE MODELLING
Year 6
Clay

5.21 LANDSCAPE MODELLING
Year 6
Clay

5.22 LOOKING AT A RIVERSIDE SCENE

5.23 MODELLING BASED ON 'THE LADY OF SHALOT'
Year 5/6
Unfired clay

5.24 MODELLING BASED ON 'THE LADY OF SHALOT'
Year 5/6
Unfired clay

5.25 MODELLING BASED ON 'THE LADY OF SHALOT'
Year 5/6
Unfired clay

art as starting points. They were looking at J W Waterhouse's painting 'The Lady of Shalot'. Together with the Lady and the boat the painting shows a stretch of water and lots of riverside foliage. So the children went to see how water and plants looked when the wind was making little waves and the plants were blowing about (figure 5.22). They made notes and sketches about the water and plants and used these in the studio to help them with their models (figures 5.22 to 5.25).

The second example shows how children used the drawings of Paul Klee and the shapes within his work to create their own landscapes (figures 5.26 to 5.28).

This kind of work is more suitable in the primary school than attempting to make pottery because the children will have insufficient skill to make pots successfully. Clay is an extremely versatile material and it helps children to use their capacity to visualise what things might look like and work out their ideas in actual forms and shapes. Making pots successfully by hand requires considerable skill and in the case of working on the wheel, quite a lot of strength. Better to encourage the children to enjoy the material and get used to making things they can handle, leaving pottery to the secondary school. If the children have learnt to love working in clay they will be keen to continue with the process later on.

5.26 LANDSCAPES BASED ON DRAWINGS BY PAUL KLEE
Year 5
Clay and glaze

5.27 LANDSCAPES BASED ON DRAWINGS BY PAUL KLEE
Year 5
Clay and glaze

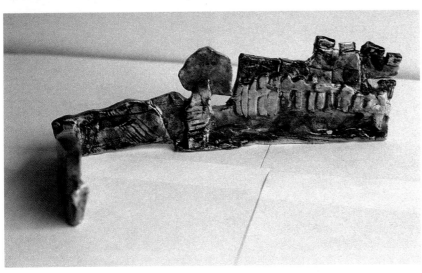

5.28 LANDSCAPES BASED ON DRAWINGS BY PAUL KLEE
Year 5
Clay and glaze

5.29   SHOE CASTS
Year 5
Plaster

5.30   SHOE SOLES IN RELIEF
Year 6
Biscuit fired clay

5.31   CARVING
Year 6
Beer stone

RIGID MATERIALS

Two opposite processes are involved here: cutting away, as in carving; or adding to, as in modelling. This is illustrated by the way the two foot-prints in figures 5.29 and 5.30 have been made, one using plaster, the other clay. The other process which uses cutting away is in print making, when blocks have to be cut in polystyrene or lino.

This is the only set of processes which demands an area of the room where a certain amount of untidiness can be contained. Alternatively, it could be out of doors if your school is fortunate to have somewhere where this is possible. In the way that Technology can produce clutter and waste material, so does work of this sort. With all rigid materials the process needs planning in advance so that it does not cause any problems.

Carving

This process takes time to set up and therefore might occur only once or twice in a child's time in primary school. It is important that children understand how sculptures can be made from stone and wood, by cutting away the outside to find a new shape within the block. To begin with, you might use small blocks of household soap or salt, or hard clay formed into a small block and left to harden in the cool. These do not need sharp tools so are suitable for younger children.

Soft stone or building blocks may be available to you in your locality. For example, the stone used in figure 5.31 was collected free from the stone mason's yard at the cathedral, when the children made a visit to see how repairs to the stonework were carried out. Carving in stone does require proper tools and, as with activities in Technology, it is important that the children have an opportunity to learn correct ways of using them.

Modroc

This is a plaster-impregnated bandage, as used in hospital for binding broken legs. It is a versatile material which you can use to make masks, or models on a small or large scale. You begin with an 'armature' or framework, in wire netting, crumpled newspaper or even a balloon and wrap the moistened bandage over it. When set, it is permanent.

Wire

Soft milliners' or flower arrangers' wire is used to wind and bend to make small models (figure 5.32). These can either be left as they are or covered in another material.

5.32 TREE SCULPTURE
Year 5
Wire

CONSTRUCTION

The variety of materials available for use here is almost endless. Egg-boxes and cardboard rolls are everyday items in use in many schools, so this section hopes to introduce some new ideas for using a variety of ordinary materials within the context of design; that is, in ways which require some pre-planning and have a definite purpose behind their construction.

Newspaper

Conventional papier mâché uses torn-up paper soaked in wallpaper paste and modelled like clay. The drawback of this method is the drying time. Models have to left for days before further work can be done or they can be painted. A more flexible method is to crumple newspaper firmly, until you have made a basic shape, hold it lightly in place with masking tape, then cover it with strips of newspaper, brushed with wallpaper paste or PVA. Once firm, it can be painted or textured to make the finished model. This method gives children the opportunity to make large structures which are not too heavy (figure 5.33).

5.33 BADGERS
Year 4/5
Papier mâché, paint and broom bristles

5.34 LANDSCAPE
Year 5/6
Folded card and watercolour

5.35 LANDSCAPES
Year 5/6
Folded card and watercolour

Card

Card can be used, folded, as a supporting structure or, uncoloured, for paper sculpture. It provides a good medium for constructing three-dimensional shapes, either very simply folded or built into box form. In the examples here the children had been looking at the work of Manet and Rousseau (one of whose works appears in the Resource Pack – no. 1). They chose the painting they thought would make the best three-dimensional work and folded and cut the card to show a foreground, middle distance and background. They copied each section they had identified on to the three layers of the card and then worked on all the blank areas of the card in a style to match the artists' work but inventing the scene for themselves (figures 5.34 and 5.35). The brief for this part of the work was that there must be a 'hidden' surprise, in character, in some part of the card.

Also using card, box structures can be made based on nets designed in the maths lesson. One example is based on the Nativity with the children's own ideas of what they wished to include. This 'diorama' format can be very successful for individual or group work with festivals or any storytelling theme (figure 5.36). The other took the form of theme boxes where each child chose to create a story box, decorating the outside with pictures of what was happening and filling the inside with suitable cut-outs on the theme of the story (figure 5.37).

With all of these projects it is important that children are involved in discussion, planning, designing and interaction.

5.36 NATIVITY SCENE
Year 5/6
Cardboard, powder colour and cut-out pictures

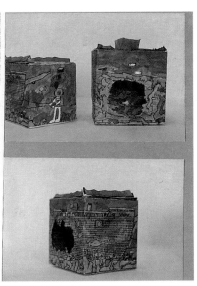

5.37 THEME BOX
Year 6
Card and watercolour

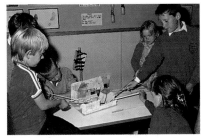

5.38 MANIPULATING THE MODEL

5.39 BIRD MASK
Year 6
Paper, card and powder colour

5.40   BIRD MASK
Year 6
Sugar paper, card and chalk

5.41   BIRD MASK
Year 6
Paper, card and powder colour

Masks

Masks are often made in association with a school production. This gives the activity a valuable focus. Many important skills can be learnt: not just the mechanical ones of cutting, forming, joining and painting. Children can be encouraged to think about character, expression and impact and how to design a mask which can be worn effectively without hampering the actor's movements or speech. It is also worth remembering at the design stage that as the actors move across the stage the mask will be seen from all round, not just from the front – so it does have to be a truly three-dimensional construction. In these examples we are looking at masks produced for some dance work, based on a Chinese story about some birds (figures 5.39 to 5.41).

Puppets

Puppets are also popular in the primary school. The earliest puppets came from ancient Greece and Rome. They were rod puppets made of terracotta and were found in tombs. Aristotle mentions a play performed with puppets in one of his plays. Shadow puppets were invented in China in the first century BC and in the 10th century Kugutsu players toured Japan performing plays using puppets. Traditional Burmese puppet marionettes can have up to 60 strings!

From these early beginnings, the history of puppetry makes fascinating reading – right up to the 'Muppets' and 'Spitting Images' puppets. Puppets are made and used in many parts of the world.

There are many sorts of puppets which use different systems to animate them. They range from paper plate and glove puppets, rod and shadow puppets, to the more sophisticated marionettes. In the primary school, puppets have functions far beyond the making of them. They are a means of communication and extending language. Children, right from their early years, are often able to express ideas and overcome difficulties such as shyness using puppets to do their talking for them. They offer an intermediary between the child, friends and teacher. Since the communication side of puppetry is so important, a good ratio for planning time is to use a quarter on making and three-quarters on using the puppets.

Just as a child will often choose the box to play with rather than the expensive toy, so basic and simple puppets may be easier to identify with. Of course they must be comfortable to use, should fit the hand, finger or arm and be of a scale to suit the size of the children in the class (figures 5.42 and 5.43). The most important use of puppets is in their contribution to oral language but plays, written and performed by the children, can also play a part in their development. In performances, audience participation is important with interaction between audience and puppets making for a richer experience.

5.42 WORKING WITH GLOVE PUPPETS
Year 1

5.43 PAPERBAG MARIONETTES
Years 4/6
Mixed media

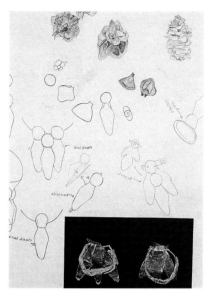

5.44 JEWELLERY DESIGN SHEETS
Year 6
Pencil, foil, thread and wire

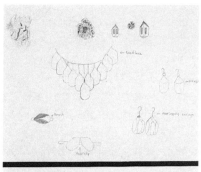
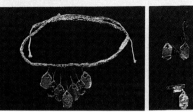

5.45 JEWELLERY DESIGN SHEETS
Year 6
Pencil, foil, thread and wire

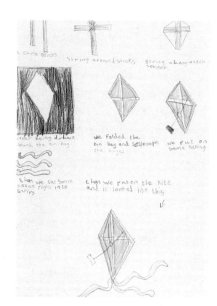

5.46 KITE DESIGNS
Year 4
Pencil, crayons and ink

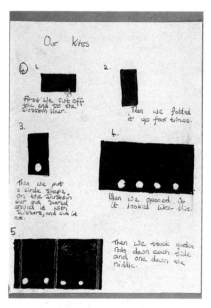

5.47 KITE DESIGNS
Year 4
Pencil, crayons and ink

Jewellery

Personal adornment has always been important and is very interesting to design. The starting points can be as varied as the shapes of petals on flowers, leaves or sections from a fir cone, shells or indeed any small object of interest to the children. Beginning, for example, with the fir cone they can make detailed drawings, showing how each section looks, then go on to use the shape to design and make earrings, brooches and necklaces (figures 5.44 and 5.45).

Kites

There are many instruction books for kite making. Flying them is proof that the design work has succeeded. Again, in this example, the children set out to draw designs for kites so that other children in the group would be able to make them. It was important to make and test a prototype so that the design could be modified or refined in the light of the kite's performance (figures 5.46 to 5.48).

A DESIGN-BASED PROJECT

The work illustrated in this section came from a week's residential course with a landscape artist in residence. The children were from a city school and the open landscape around the residential centre was unfamiliar to many of them. They began by exploring the area and finding out as much as they could about the countryside. The artist took them for a walk and pointed out all the things he would look for in order to make a painting. He described how he would make visual notes about the appearance of things he might want to use in a painting and how he would write notes about colours and other details that interested him. Then he began some preliminary sketches and the children watched.

One of the many advantages of visiting a residential centre is that work can continue all day without the need to change every hour or two to a different activity. The children used drawing boards (made out of strawboard for lightness), and pegs to hold the paper in place. They went out to draw in the environment, to make sketches for later work in the studio (figures 5.49 and 5.50). They took cameras with them, too, to record things of special interest that they might want to use later (figure 5.51).

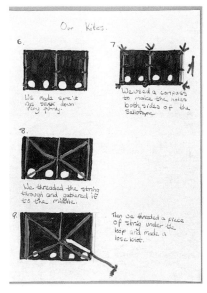

5.48 KITE DESIGNS
Year 4
Pencil, crayons and ink

5.49 LANDSCAPE DRAWINGS
Year 6
Pencil and charcoal

5.51 LANDSCAPE PHOTOGRAPH

5.50 LANDSCAPE DRAWINGS
Year 6
Pencil and charcoal

The next stage in the project was to record the landscape in colour and detail in the form of a painting, made from the sketches and information gathered on their walks (figure 5.52). Then, to use the opportunities offered at the centre to work in two- and three-dimensional design, the children chose to carry their work on into textiles or ceramics. As in an earlier example, they were able to select an area they felt could be carried on into other forms by 'keyholing' an area of their painting. Some children chose to look specifically at the colours in the landscape, some at the intricate details in trees, hedges and farm buildings – each child making a personal record of things they had found that meant most to them. This completed the time spent on the art and design aspects of the residential work.

Back at school, weavings were completed and ceramics fired, coloured and glazed. Then the sections of weaving and ceramic were laid out on the floor and joined with plaited yarns into a wall hanging (figures 5.53 and 5.54).

Work on this scale needs a great deal of planning and the opportunity to work together over a period of time. Experience in a residential centre is valuable in many ways and this particular work illustrates how extremely successful it can be. The children took immense pleasure in what they had produced and appreciated that these sorts of activities need time and effort. It changed their outlook and enabled them to continue to produce work of a high order.

5.52 LANDSCAPE PAINTING
Year 6
Tempera

5.53 LANDSCAPE WALL HANGING
Year 6
Mixed media

5.54 LANDSCAPE WALL HANGING
Year 6
Mixed media

6 Reflection and assessment

6.1   DISCUSSIONS ABOUT THE WORK

REFLECTION AND ASSESSMENT

Assessment and review are covered more fully in *Principles and Practice in Art*, so here we will look at them in relation to investigating and making. The National Curriculum requires children to be assessed at the end of each Key Stage. You also need to keep a record of their progress to assist you in reporting to parents. It is important to remember that assessment is not done in isolation, with a decision having to be made about a single piece of work. You should have most of a child's work to look at and assess alongside that of others. The assessments you make should be the end result of a process that has continued throughout the year. The decisions you reach will be based on the work in front of you, supported by your understanding of it, gained through talking with each child (figure 6.1).

Children need to reflect on their work and to share in assessment. It helps if this can become an accepted part of their work, so that they are looking at their own progress and making their own assessments about what they are learning. They will also be finding out more about themselves and their needs and achievements.

6.2 TALKING ABOUT WHERE TO GO NEXT

With all research and investigation there should be a continuing dialogue. You will want to discuss with the child how much has been learnt, the ways in which it has been recorded and where it is to go next. In talking about their work children can explain what they are trying to achieve. You will find out what sort of help or support they need in order to carry it forward successfully (figure 6.2). One way in which you can assess children's ability to research and investigate is to see how far beyond the original brief they can go. The wider the scope of their enquiry, the more ways they have found of approaching the subject. The more selective they have been about the tools and materials they have used, the higher the level of achievement in this aspect of their work.

Making poses different challenges. As we know, within each group of children there is a range of ability. In assessing work, therefore, you should look at the genuine attempt to satisfy the task they were given. For example, if a painting is competent and shows ability in handling materials, the thoroughness of the research should match it – if it is to qualify for a particular level of achievement.

Levels of achievement are arrived at through your experience of looking at lots of children's work. You will find that when you and your colleagues look at work together, the relative stages of development become clear. You need to be looking for indicators like:

– How well is the object placed on the paper?
– How carefully have the details been drawn?
– How well was the child able to handle the tools and equipment?

In the following examples you will see how the balance of discussion and looking form the basis of an overall assessment of achievement.

TALKING ABOUT THE WORK

Children learn from many sources. In Art and Design they will already have some knowledge when they come to you. Encourage them to share that knowledge and help them all to contribute by asking them questions about the sort of things they enjoy drawing and painting, which tools they like to use best and why. When they are used to making a contribution to classroom discussion, plan to have time to do this at the end of each lesson. Instead of finishing with clearing up, do that first and keep the final 10 minutes for sharing what has been done and planning what might come next. The discussion can begin by looking at the work, asking the children how well they thought they had achieved what they set out to do and how well they had used their time. These are some of the sort of questions you need to ask:

- Were you making it for yourself or to be of interest and value to others, or both?
- What have you learned that was new to you?
- Have you thoroughly explored the tools and materials and made best use of them?
- What changes might you make if you did this again?
- How effectively have you used your time? (For example, children work at different speeds and need to be aware how much they are achieving in a lesson.)
- What qualities does the finished piece of work have and to what extent did its success depend on the thoroughness of the investigation and research that led up to it?

Ask them to reflect on the wider purpose of making things and discuss how what they have been doing fits into the world outside school.

In this sort of discussion with older children you will have laid the foundations of a critical awareness of their own work in a wider context. You can go on to help the children to address questions like 'What sort of qualities are evident in your work and do they mean the same thing to others as to the person who made them?' Both you and they will find it useful to note down what has been discussed so next time you can start by remembering what happened in the work last time.

LOOKING AT DRAWINGS

Children develop at different rates and will be able to tackle more complex subjects as they gain experience. As well as their own natural ability we need to remember that how well they do depends, to some extent, on the experience of the subject they have had so far. What sort of progress they have made and how much they enjoy the subject will depend on how well the tasks they were given in the past matched their needs at each stage. In assessing a Level of Attainment, as with all testing, we have to measure the child's achievement at a given time and not take into consideration the sort of background they have had. We need to look at how well they have performed in the work they have been given. We need to be able to see how well the children have understood what they had to do and how much their work tells us about what they understand and can do.

In the end of Key Stage Statements for making we are asked to base our assessments on:

— how well children have been able to handle tools and materials;
— how competent they are in using and understanding the visual language of art and design;
— how effectively they can talk about their work, recognise the need to make changes and modify their original ideas.

As they progress through each level the basic requirements remain the same but become more complex in terms of understanding, knowledge and self evaluation.

In order to illustrate the sort of things you might look for in a series of drawings, this example shows the work of children from a mixed class of Years 1 and 2. The variation in development is therefore across age as well as ability giving a fairly wide spread. You need to know what the children were asked to do in order to understand what to look for in assessing the level of the drawings. The task for these children was to make a drawing of a stuffed Light Sussex cockerel, borrowed from the local resources service (figures 6.3 and 6.4). They were given oil pastels and black sugar paper and asked to begin by making all the colours they could see in the bird – his eyes, beak, comb and feathers (figure 6.5).

6.3 & 6.4 MAKING DRAWINGS FROM THE COCKEREL
Years 1 and 2
Oil pastel

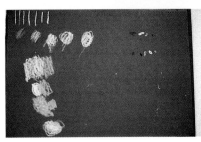

6.5 MAKING THE COLOURS SEEN IN THE COCKEREL
Years 1 and 2
Oil pastel

**6.6   DRAWING OF THE
COCKEREL**
Year 1
Oil pastel

**6.7–6.10   DRAWINGS OF THE
COCKEREL**
Years 1 and 2
Oil pastel

In the five drawings illustrated (figures 6.6 to 6.10) we can see the gradual change in perception that takes place. In the first one the child was interested in the overall shape and colour of the bird (figure 6.6). It is drawn with care, using the colours in blocks. Like work done in the early years, the bird's feet are resting on the edge or baseline of the paper, which is used to stand for the ground. It is recognisable as the bird but could benefit from more definition and awareness of detail. In the second and subsequent drawings you can see that the bird is placed more in the centre of the paper, to allow for other things to be put around it if needed (figures 6.7 to 6.10). As you look at each drawing you can see how the child has made a conscious effort to place legs and feet in the correct place under the bird and to get the relative proportions right. Then they have looked for line, pattern and detail and begun to make the pastel marks follow the direction of the feathers. There is also an attempt to show an element of 'character'.

In each subsequent drawing you can see how the bird not only becomes more recognisable but the details become more defined and the different parts of the bird are in better proportion to each other. For example, in the first drawings, feet, heads and tails are about the same size, whereas in the later ones they are drawn more like their real size compared with each other.

LOOKING AT PAINTINGS

By continuing to look at children's pictures of birds you can see that different criteria need to be used to assess these paintings. One task with Year 6 children was to work from observation and the imagination, to make a painting of the bird and set it in some appropriate context (figure 6.11). In these examples all the criteria used to study the drawings apply – those of position, size and scale and handling of the materials. Over and above these things we also need to look at how paint and colour have been used. The criteria you would base your assessment on are not only more detailed but also take into consideration how sensitively the materials have been handled (figures 6.12 to 6.15).

For example, in the painting of the bird you can see line, shape and attention to detail and in the handling of the paint you can see texture, tone and colour. How much has each child seen and how well have they been able to use their skill in handling the paint and colour? We looked earlier, in chapter 3, at how light tones in the background help to make the subject of the painting more prominent. We also saw how paintings are built up in layers of paint and how important the direction of the brush marks can be. The four examples (figures 6.12 to 6.15) are all of interest because they illustrate a growing understanding of the importance of these points. Each one is valid in its own right but each shows a greater ability to handle shape, form and colour.

With practice in looking at work like this you will be able to pick out the things which indicate where, in any set of work, each piece belongs.

6.11 VULTURE BORROWED FROM THE MUSEUM

6.12–6.15 PAINTINGS OF THE VULTURE
Year 6
Tempera

If you look back at figure 6.10 and compare it with figure 6.12 you can see how much more there is in terms of overall sensitivity to shape, and the detail is far more defined. There is more of an element of composition, even greater attention to the shape and character of the bird and a definite sense of it's place standing within the picture. In the next painting you can see all of the previous qualities but here the use of paint and colour gives far more information than in the previous paintings. Compared with the actual bird, figure 6.11, you get a real sense of a painting having been made, using the bird as a starting point.

Just as in Year 6, some children are reading well above the average, so some are able to go far beyond what is usual for their age group in understanding and making in art and design. The last of the vulture paintings has all of the qualities discussed previously but in addition shows real ability in handling paint, colour, form and composition. The overall shape of the bird together with the way that the line and pattern have been painted reflect a mature approach to the subject. It is important to recognise that work of this nature can be produced where the children have had a good experience in art and design throughout their years in primary school. It is equally important to ensure that they are given sufficiently challenging work to allow them to continue to make further headway. Where there are children of above average ability in the class others will benefit from a more informed discussion, and they will see how tasks are tackled by those with more sophisticated abilities.

ASSESSING TWO- AND THREE-DIMENSIONAL WORK

Assessing work in two and three dimensions needs to take account of children's ability to handle tools and materials sensitively as well as to draw in many different media. In each craft area you will be looking for the way they have understood the process and how well they have matched the lines, shapes and forms of their designs to the materials they are using. It is important to be able to draw well in order to be successful in any craft, but that does not necessarily mean drawing on paper. It can refer to drawing well in the material itself, for example, with a pointed tool into a printing block or drawing three dimensionally in clay with hands and tools. It is also important to look for evidence that the children have understood the process, not simply followed instructions on how to make a piece of work. In any learning situation, the object is not to produce an end result but to enable the children to learn the process so that they can go on to design and make things for themselves and others, using the process as another way of expressing ideas. You need to take this aspect of their work into account.

In your assessment of these different areas some of the criteria will be common to each of the crafts. These are the child's attitude to the work, how sensitively tools and materials are handled and how effectively has the process been used.

Each of the crafts also has its own special skills and these need to be understood, too. For example, in print making the lines and patterns need to fill and enhance the shapes, in clay the patterns and textures need to follow the form. In the following examples you will see how two different craft areas can be assessed using similar criteria, related to the individual materials.

Print making

The prints of fish were made after making drawings of real fish and comparing them with some Victorian steel engravings of fish from a book on identifying different species. The children looked at the overall shape and outline to start with, then at the series of lines and patterns which filled the shape. They used the card block method of printing and drew into the surface with a variety of sharp points in different thicknesses. All of the prints are good and have been chosen for this example because the differences between them are small (figures 6.16 to 6.19). The things you would look for are:

● The outline is definitely fish shaped but does it tell us as clearly, in each print, which sort of fish it is?
● How carefully have the patterns been observed and drawn?
● The pattern may have been drawn with care, but does it fit around the fish well?
● How many different sorts of pattern have been seen and how many different types of tools have been used to make those accurately?
● How clearly has the print come out or are there any 'thin' patches in the colour?

6.16–6.19 PRINTS MADE FROM LOOKING AT FISH
Year 6
Water-based printing ink

These same questions are relevant to all print making. You need only change the subject matter to relate to what has been drawn or depicted in the print.

In these examples you can see how the five criteria outlined above can be applied to the fish in the prints. The first prints are fish shaped, have different areas of pattern and have been fairly carefully observed. These are followed by a drawing where the details have been drawn more sensitively and individual areas of pattern carefully delineated. The spines and fins are more interestingly drawn to give a patterned quality to the outline of the fish. In the last print we can see all the previous features, again drawn with greater skill in understanding how to use this process to advantage; fine lines, an interesting outline, contrasting areas of plain and pattern making for a good, clear print.

Working with clay

In working with clay the questions are similar but relate essentially to the three-dimensional nature of the work. As the examples are again fish you will be able to compare the two sets of illustrations to see how the same subject matter can be used effectively in two craft areas. The children here had been given a plate of herrings to work from and could choose how many fish they wanted to make (figures 6.20 to 6.23). In assessing the work you would be looking at the following:

● How does the width and thickness of the fish vary along its length?
● How is the fish arranged in relation to the plate?
● Does the plate have a three-dimensional shape or is it flat?
● How well defined are the head, tail and fins and are they in the right places?
● Have the patterns of scales, gills and fins been sensitively modelled?

In the first two examples you can see different qualities in each piece of work. One shows the fish have been made well enough to look fish shaped and have been overlapped in a realistic way. In the other the fish are still flat but they are a good shape, the tails and scales are clearly shown and the plate has an edge. In the next example the work is essentially more three dimensional, although there is not a great deal of pattern the fish are round and solid and go well together as a group on the plate. The last example shows a more considered composition. The fish have pattern, shape and solidity, the lemon is sensitively modelled and the plate fits the design.

**6.20–6.23 CLAY MODELS BASED
ON FISH**
Years 5 and 6
Biscuit fired clay

One overall question which refers to both examples would be what sort of impact does it make and how interesting is it? In fabric and textile work you would be looking for comparable indications of skill and understanding such as use of tools and materials and an increasingly well researched design together with developing skill in making. Other two and three dimensional crafts can be assessed in the same way, by looking for indications of the increasing competence and understanding in the work and by seeing how well the children have coped with the actual tasks they were given. These are the sort of questions which we can ask about work in all craft areas. They are in addition to those questions outlined at the beginning, about understanding why it is important to design and make things, how to communicate through our work and how to use tools, equipment and materials sensitively.

7 Choosing and managing materials and equipment

7.1 MAKING A DRAWING WITH A PENCIL

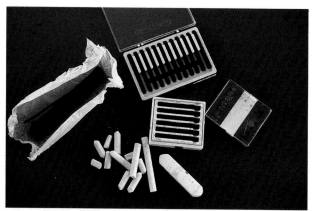

7.2 CHALK, CHARCOAL AND CONTE

CHOOSING A RANGE OF MATERIALS

Comprehensive lists of tools, equipment and materials are available in the catalogues offered by the major art equipment suppliers. Each section offers a range of materials. By comparing one catalogue with another you will be able to see what opportunities there are and how expensive it will be to equip your room or school to handle drawing, painting and design. You need to choose equipment and materials that will provide a range of experiences for the children through their seven years in the primary school. When you plan your art curriculum to deliver the Programmes of Study remember that you need to give the children different experiences in some depth — in drawing, painting and one or possibly two areas of design each year. You should try to match the times when children study different skills to when they are with members of staff who have some expertise in the craft areas they are going to teach.

Materials are mentioned in some detail in chapters 2 and 3, where distinctions have been made between the various ways in which they can be used. Here they are listed in their relative importance and suggestions are made as to which ones you should buy.

Drawing

Children need to draw, using a wide variety of tools on different surfaces, throughout each year. Drawing, in all its forms, is the most important activity and the one from which all the other art activities grow. You should try to acquire a wide range of mark-making implements so that the children become conversant with their many different qualities.

Pencils need to be bought in three grades — HB, 2B and 4B or 6B — or at least an equivalent range (figure 7.1). Charcoal pencils are available and can be useful but they need to be sharpened with care — they break easily compared with ordinary lead pencils.

Chalk and charcoal are important because they can be blended so easily and will smudge into each other to create tones (figure 7.2). They should be used in their own right and as a contrast to things which produce fine, crisp lines. Conte is a black crayon which is square in section. The shape permits you to use it for lettering as well as for drawing. Conte is more expensive than charcoal but it does produce a different effect so it is useful to have a box or two for the children to try.

You should have some biros which are excellent for line drawing and sketching. Because you cannot rub them out they demand a certain sort of concentration. However, you should remember that biro ink is not light fast, so any work you have on display will fade. Fibre tip pens use a more permanent type of ink so drawings should last indefinitely, but this will depend on each manufacturer's method of producing the ink. For a guaranteed permanent ink you would have to buy specialist drawing inks used in artists' or architects' 'valve' type pens.

7.3   DRAWING FROM OBSERVATION
Year 1/2
Oil pastel

7.4   TWO TYPES OF COLOURED PENCIL

In coloured drawing tools you need a range which might include wax crayons, chalk pastels, oil pastels (figure 7.3) and coloured pencils (figure 7.4). Many of these types of crayons and pastels are sold in packets of mixed colours but it is better, and more economical, to buy boxes of single colours, especially in oil pastels.

Here, as in all the materials you have, it is better to buy a smaller range of better quality than to try to have some of all that is available. Faced with a limited budget you should try to have the three grades of pencils, biros and/or fibre tip pens, wax crayons, oil pastels and a few coloured pencils – to experience the characteristic qualities of the different marks they can make.

Painting

All children need to have experience in paint and here they should be using powder colour because it is the most flexible medium for colour mixing. In **Key Stage 1**, paint is often mixed for children to use straight from the pot because they are drawing with paint rather than using it as a medium to explore for its own sake (figure 7.5). However, when the children are mixing their own colours they need to have access to pots of dry colour so that they can experiment and learn how to mix and make colours for themselves (figures 7.6 and 7.7).

Next you would introduce watercolours, predominantly in **Key Stage 2** (figure 7.8). Watercolours, like biro drawings, should not be hung where

7.5 POWDER COLOURS MIXED FOR PAINTING

7.6 POWDER COLOUR STORAGE

7.7 POWDER COLOUR STORAGE

where there is bright sunlight because some of the colours are what is known as 'fugitive' and will fade in time.

Another colour medium you might use are coloured inks, used in the way in which you might use watercolours, to make coloured drawings and to colour illustrations. As with watercolours, they should not be hung in direct sunlight.

In readymix paint it is useful to have some black, as mentioned in chapter 3, to use with powder colour. You may also want to have the primary colours in readymix, for large-scale work where you may need to mix bigger quantities, such as for painting big models or scenery. Here again, it is important to have a range of paint so that children are in a position to compare the effects they can achieve with each type.

When you are ordering crayons or paint, always buy twice as much white and yellow as you do of the other colours as these will be used up more quickly.

7.8 WORKING WITH WATERCOLOUR
Year 4

7.9 MAKING A PAINTING
Year 3

Papers

Quality is even more important here. Paper is sold not only by sizes, which you will find in the catalogues, but by weight. The heavier the paper the firmer and more solid it will be. Light papers are alright to use with dry media to make sketches or quick drawings in pencil or biro. For detailed drawing, where the quality of the mark is important, you should use a heavier paper so that the children can see and learn to control the marks they are making. For example, cartridge paper gives a good, flat surface for pencil, pen or brush drawing; medium grade sugar paper is excellent for chalk, charcoal, wax crayons or pastels; for coloured pencils, cartridge is again the best as the colours will show up with more brilliance. (Though it must be said that using coloured pencils on dark sugar paper can produce some unusual effects.)

Kitchen paper or 'Junior art' paper will not take paint. It goes soggy and the colours disappear into it. With powder colour or readymix, use cartridge or coloured sugar papers (figure 7.9) and cartridge paper for watercolour.

Brushes

These are mentioned in chapter 3. It is best to buy nylon filament brushes: size 2 or 02 is a very fine one and you need a few of these for detailed work. Sizes 4, 6 and 8 would give a good range for everyday use with watercolour or detail work in powder colour. In long-handled brushes you should have a choice of either small, medium and large, or 6, 10 and 12. In addition, you might buy two or three decorators' brushes, in 25 mm or 50 mm, for making a colour wash.

Two-dimensional design

When you have chosen which areas of two-dimensional design to study, buy a limited range to begin with and build it up over a few years.

The materials you need for print making consist of water-based inks, firm and absorbent paper like cartridge paper and the best rollers you can afford. The ones made of gelatine are excellent because they are flat and resilient and will produce an even print. You should also have some metal spoons for burnishing prints, that is, to rub over the back of the paper to make a clear print.

In textiles you will need to buy fabrics, both to print on and for batik; whereas for weaving you can collect threads and scrap materials. The dyes you buy should be those that are easily 'fixed', that is made permanent by ironing. Those which fade or run can cause disappointment. For batik it is best to buy the purpose-made wax; candles will melt down but the wax does not flow evenly and can be difficult to handle and control.

In Information Technology you will need to buy whatever your computer requires in the way of papers and coloured inks, but bear in mind that the colours of most inks will fade if they are hung on the wall, even if not in sunlight.

Three-dimensional design

Plastic materials such as clay need to be bought locally, because of their weight, now that transport costs are so high. Glazes, coloured glazes, slips, stains and oxides are best bought from the same supplier as they should then all be compatible. Plastic modelling tools are useful. Wooden ones are more expensive but have a different feel and it is helpful to have both. Plastic clay knives are safer than the metal ones. You will need wires for cutting clay and wooden rolling pins and rolling guides for tile making. You can also make use of all sorts of found objects to print and shape clay – particularly useful are old cheese graters or Surform blades which you can use to smooth or 'grate' the clay into strands to use for grass and other textures.

Rigid materials include plaster and modroc, both of which require a framework to build on. You can use newspaper for small structures but for larger models wire netting or chicken wire will be needed to provide a firm base.

The children can be encouraged to save and collect all cardboard and plastic forms for construction, though 'junk' modelling needs to be handled with care. Although it is easy to do and to resource, it is not necessarily a valuable exercise. This kind of activity is probably best explored in Technology where modelling is allied to the skills of shaping, joining, designing and building. One good use for found and collected materials is puppet making where you will need to have access to a wide range of fabrics, papers, card, string, threads and paint.

Other materials like stone and brick depend on local sources and probably will only be used from time to time in connection with a specific project.

CHOOSING EQUIPMENT

This is a more complicated area to discuss than materials because you will be dependent, to some extent, on space when it comes to choosing which two- and three-dimensional crafts you can include successfully. Following the outline of the previous section on materials we can look at the equipment you might need to support work in the different areas.

For drawing and painting you need to have drawing boards. Wooden ones are best as they can be used for support and also to 'stretch' paper for watercolour painting. To do this you make a sheet of cartridge paper damp and then stick it on to the board with brown paper tape. It needs to dry slowly, away from any heat. When dried it can be used for painting and will remain flat. This is a substitute for the more expensive watercolour paper or board which artists use.

For most methods of print making you need only a flat area of plate glass or formica to roll ink on to but a press is useful if you want to make lino prints.

Fabric printing with a block can be done on a large, flat table, but to screen print a length of fabric you need a print table covered in american cloth so that the fabric can be fixed firmly. Both silk screen and batik work require frames on which to stretch the fabric. You could buy a basic range of screens or frames and see if it is possible to improvise to make some more. Old picture frames can be adapted into frames for batik and silk screen frames can be made from cardboard boxes. However, it is important for safety reasons to have a purpose-made waxpot for batik work. You can now buy a small, inexpensive and well-designed model which is self-contained and safe.

Although clay work does not depend on having a kiln, if one can be used it completes the process. The newer fibre-insulated, top-loading kilns are ideal for school use; less expensive to buy and run than conventional brick, front-loading kilns. They can run from a 13-amp outlet and are portable. A pottery wheel is not necessary in primary work and better left to the secondary school where the children will have more strength and the patience to persist.

MANAGEMENT AND STORAGE

In organising your room or art area you need to equip it with a variety of containers. Baskets from the supermarket, in different colours, make it easy for the children to have access to the materials and equipment when they need them (figures 7.10 to 7.12). By choosing a range of colours for different curriculum areas you can make it easy to identify what things belong to each subject. Simple shelving can be made to accommodate the storage baskets and leave your sink area and some of the working surfaces free (figures 7.13 and 7.14).

Other containers you need to have are screwtop jars to keep dyes safely, 2-litre icecream boxes to store glazes, bowls and jugs for measuring and racks to store sets of pencils and brushes (figure 7.15). A large plastic dustbin will hold the clay satisfactorily but will be even better if you can take a little time to prepare it. House bricks are absorbent and will hold water. Find some whole bricks to fill the base of the dustbin and

7.10 STORAGE BASKETS AND SHELVING

7.11 STORAGE BASKETS AND SHELVING

7.12 STORAGE BASKETS AND SHELVING

7.13 STORAGE AROUND THE SINK AREA

7.14 COLOUR CODED STORAGE

7.15   PENS, PENCILS AND TOOLS IN STORAGE RACKS

cut a few others to complete the base so that it forms a flat surface. Lay some sacking or hessian over the brick base and tuck it firmly down the sides. Pour some water down the side of the bin so that the bricks are moist. This will keep the atmosphere in the bin damp and the clay will not dry out, no matter how long it is left. When the clay is first delivered, cut it into squares and roll these into 'tennis ball' sized pieces. Put these gently into the bin and cover with more damp hessian. Managed like this the children will only have to lift out one or two balls of clay each time they use it. Ensure that at the end of a lesson they roll up all spare clay into balls and it can go straight back into the bin for use next time.

USING BASIC EQUIPMENT

Magnifying glasses are useful as focusing devices and for drawing from observation. It is useful to have both individual, hand-held ones and a few of those on stands, leaving hands free for drawing (figures 7.16 and 7.17).

Viewfinders are important and usually made in school. They are made out of medium black or white card and can be cut to any shape to match the sort of work or to give an unusual shape to the drawing or painting (figure 7.18).

Mirrors and mirror packs, which are used in Science, are helpful for drawing self-portraits, either straight or distorted. They are also useful for checking what printing blocks will turn out like when they have been printed.

A cutting mat is invaluable and, though expensive to buy, will be a tremendous asset. It provides an excellent surface for cutting on, but more than that, because of the texture of their surface, they actually seem to hold what you are cutting in place. Use this when you are making your viewfinders!

Drawing boards make it possible for children to work on a sloping surface. They will find this helpful for observational drawing, when they have to look up to see the model or object. A drawing board also provides a personal space and can actually add to the working surface where table space is limited (figures 7.19 and 7.20).

Not essential but very useful if you have space is a light box. This provides a glass or plastic surface with a light underneath, on which you can view slides or any delicate object like leaf skeletons or flower petals.

COLLECTING FOR CRAFT WORK

Children can be their own best resource providers and need to be encouraged to contribute to displays of all kinds of two- and three-dimensional work. Collecting is a hobby for many adults as well as children. In the classroom it needs to be focused, as suggested in chapter 5, on one or more aspect of work at a time. You might choose to focus on different crafts or look at the same subject matter to see how it can be treated in different ways.

7.16   USING MAGNIFYING GLASSES

7.17 USING MAGNIFYING GLASSES

7.18 USING A VIEWFINDER
Year 6

7.19 USING DRAWING BOARDS
Year 5

7.20 USING DRAWING BOARDS
Year 5

The collection can include magazine and comic illustrations, photographs, postcards of works of art and pictures the children like or find interesting.

Catalogues from exhibitions you have visited together often contain useful illustrations, as do posters from exhibitions like those at the Royal Academy, the Tate and the Yorkshire Sculpture Park. In Part 1 there is a list of other places from which you might collect information and illustrations of all kinds (page 98).

HEALTH AND SAFETY

Most manufacturers now provide non-toxic materials for school use. Pottery suppliers do have poisonous substances in their catalogues but these are clearly marked and should not be bought. Most inks and dyes are safe but all substances need to be handled and stored with care and this should be a part of the learning process.

Most schools have their own policy on what they will accept in terms of equipment. The choice, for instance, between sharp pointed and round bladed scissors is one which the majority of schools would decide for themselves. Many take the view that children need to learn how to handle the tools and equipment which are appropriate to each area of the curriculum, under careful supervision and with guidance.

Your County Education Department may have documents and publications on Health and Safety in Art and Design. If so, these should be displayed in your classroom or art area, or in the case of pottery by the kiln. There should also be a first aid box that is easily accessible.

As well as safety information, many suppliers' catalogues give invaluable advice about glues, paints and dyes and what to do if they are spilt or come into contact with clothing. This is often in the form of a chart and it would be well worth keeping a copy in your classroom.

Bibliography

Part 1 Investigating in art

AAiAD, *Learning through Drawing* (AAiAD 1976)

Clement, R T, *The Art Teacher's Handbook* (Hutchinson 1986)

Clement, R T, *A Framework for Art, Craft and Design in the Primary School* (Devon LEA 1990)

Devon County Council, *Young Children's Learning* (Devon LEA 1990)

DES, *Art in Junior Education* (HMSO 1978)

Gentle, K, *Children and Art Teaching* (Croom Helm 1985)

NSEAD, *Art, Craft and Design in the Primary School* (NSEAD 1986)

Morgan, M and Page, S, *Supplement for Primary Teachers* (The Open College of the Arts)

Robertson, S, *Rosegarden and Labyrinth* (RKP)

Schools Council, *Art 7–11* (Schools Council 1978)

Schools Council, *Resources for Visual Education* (Schools Council 1978)

Part 2 Making in art

AAiAD, *Learning through Drawing* (AAiAD 1976)

Adams, E and Ward, C, *Art and the Built Environment* (Longman 1982)

Arnheim, R, *Art and Visual Perception* (Faber 1967)

Barrett, M, *Art Education: A Strategy for Course Design* (Heinemann 1980)

Clement, R T, *The Art Teacher's Handbook* (Hutchinson 1986)

Clement, R T, *A Framework for Art, Craft and Design in the Primary School* (Devon LEA 1990)

Devon County Council, *Young Children's Learning* (Devon LEA 1990)

DES, *Art in Junior Education* (HMSO 1978)

Gentle, K, *Children and Art Teaching* (Croom Helm 1985)

Gulbenkian Foundation, *The Arts in Schools* (Gulbenkian Foundation 1982)

Morgan, M and Page, S, *Supplement for Primary Teachers* (The Open College for the Arts 1990)

NSEAD, *Art, Craft and Design in the Primary School* (NSEAD 1986)

Read, H, *Education through Art* (Faber & Faber 1959)

Robertson, S, *Rosegarden and Labyrinth* (RKP)

Schools Council, *Art 7–11* (Schools Council 1978)

Schools Council, *Resources for Visual Education* (Schools Council 1978)

The Design Council, *Design and Primary Education* (The Design Council 1987)

Index

DIS LIBRARY
DANUBE INTL. SCHOOL
2 JOSEF GANGL GASSE 2
A 1020 VIENNA AUSTRIA
TEL 720 31 10 NE TEL.